THE
SINGLE
TRUTH

*Challenging
the Misconceptions
of Singleness
with God's
Consuming Truth*

LORI SMITH

DEDICATION

For the single friends who helped me find
truth—especially Kristine, Suzanna, Kate, and KC.
Our many conversations played the midwife to this book.

ACKNOWLEDGMENTS

I want to thank the many people who helped me through the slow-as-growing-coral process that was this book. My parents' support has been constant and invaluable. They taught me many of the principles here and taught me by example to speak truth in love. I hope I've succeeded in doing that. They propped me up after rejection letters and helped with the myriad details of life (thanks for the leftovers, Mom!) when I was working full-time and writing on deadline. They and the rest of my family put up with me on my bad days and saw value in this venture, encouraging me to risk and dream.

I am so thankful for my single friends (some of whom are no longer single, but well remember the single life). Many of the ideas here were birthed on weekend trips to the beach, on day trips to pick blackberries, over a slow cup of coffee or a home-cooked meal, in all the good conversations we've had.

Kristine Steakley shared my vision from the beginning, read many early chapter drafts, and provided the accountability I needed to get started. Candice McGarvey gave me the title. Mike and Rhonda Cochran and Beth and Kevin Brown launched this effort with prayer. The Thursday night Bible study was my support group in the early days; they understood what it meant to take risks to follow God and helped me ask questions and write from an appreciation of the depth and mystery of faith. Deanna and Robyn were like my own personal cheerleaders—they believed in this book and in me as a writer. The Chantilly Bible Church family lifted this up in their prayers. And my back would not have survived the stress without its frequent visits to Dr. H. and his healing hands.

Cec Murphey listened, encouraged me, and provided guidance at the Sandy Cove Communicators conference when I was ready to give up. As a new writer trying to figure out the publishing world, his insight was a lifeline. The Capital Christian Writers group showed me the ropes and cheered me on. Scott Fehrenbacher sent me to CBA with the Crosswalk.com team. Joe Battaglia introduced me to my agent, Bruce Barbour, who believed in the book and was willing to work with a first-timer. Don Milam and his team at Destiny Image provided a good home for this project.

And, of course, thanks to God who gave me this assignment and the inspiration to finish it. I am thankful that perhaps He will use my own struggles for a greater good.

CONTENTS

INTRODUCTION

❧

I spend a lot of time waiting for life to make sense.

When I was young, I knew I would grow up, go to college, fall in love, get married, and have a family. Maybe you thought the same thing.

For me, love didn't come on cue.

I graduated from college, got a job, and thought, *Now. This is when I fall in love. This must be it.*

And there have been guys—guys who couldn't dance and forgot my name and asked me if I "type and stuff" (an actual quote), because that's what women are supposed to do after all.

In all fairness, there have been some good ones, too. But none of them were right for me.

Many of my closest friends are married. They've had babies, bought houses, and settled down. Their lives make sense—at least, looking from my vantage point.

I keep working and waiting…and wondering.

To my credit, I didn't wait for a man to begin living my life. The thought of putting off something I wanted or needed to do just because I didn't have a man alongside me made me sick. It still does. So I've had good jobs, lived on my own, gone to Paris, walked on the beach, and admired every evening sky.

The older I get, though, the more intense the questioning becomes: What is God doing with my life? (What am I doing with my life?) What if I never get married?

These issues are often only in the back of my mind, and my days are full of otherwise meaningful activity. But sometimes they erupt into everyday life with tremendous emotional force. Fear, grief, and jealousy control me.

I'm facing this head-on. I expect God to give me peace and contentment now, in my singleness. I think He'll bring it Himself, not by bringing me a man. Knowing Him will be my ultimate cure.

The purpose of this book isn't to wallow in my own grief or to tell you how to catch a husband or wife (as if they could be caught, or as if a relationship based on such a catch would be worthwhile). Its purpose is to deal truthfully with singleness and its effects on our lives. I hope to identify the encumbrances that are inherent in single life—and to help us lay them aside so we can "run with endurance the race that is set before us" (Heb. 12:1 NAS).

Chapter One

LOSS

❧

"Last weekend, when I turned off the TV and had some time to think, I came to peace about something." Brian spoke slowly, but deliberately. "I came to peace with the fact that I'm just not ready to be married yet. Honestly, I just can't see myself getting married anytime in the next two years."

Brian and I had been dating for over a year. As I listened, I felt my soul pulling away, like when you drew in your breath after you skinned your knee when you were a kid. For a minute, you didn't feel any pain; you were just stunned.

A wave of grief and loneliness was building just in front of me, ready to swallow me, and I couldn't get away.

I sat there, trying to get the world to stop spinning, trying to comprehend the weight of what was just spoken.

After several minutes, I spoke, sensing that the words didn't come from me but from God. "Well, it was a good year."

"Yeah, it was a great year. It was a great year." From the look on his face, he meant every word.

Finally, the tears came. We sat in silence for a long time. I followed Brian numbly into the kitchen as he put up his glass, and then we prayed. We sat awkwardly on the stairs of the townhouse. We didn't touch, but it was enough to be there together, praying, thanking God for His blessings, grace, and guidance, asking for His strength.

"Talk to you later." With that, he shut the door. I stood there leaning against the corner for the next five minutes. I was still numb; I couldn't comprehend how I would survive the days and weeks and years that stretched bleakly in front of me.

I had never experienced that kind of pain. I felt like the foundation of my world had collapsed, and I couldn't break my fall.

That following Sunday, my pastor preached a message that seemed to be aimed directly at me. It was about the peace of God and the hope we can have in the worst situation when we know God is using it for our good, making something beautiful with it. With that message, God gave me hope that would carry me through the dark days to come. He would use this loss to carve away at my black heart and make me more like Him. Something new would be born in me—a new peace, a new humility, a more genuine love. In spite of all this—through all this—God would work good, and He would make me a little more right in the process. I held on to that promise.

I don't remember much about the next few months except that they were dark. The healing process was predictable only in the fact that it was unpredictable. I wrote in my journal:

Just when I think I'll never be done with it, I'm suddenly overwhelmed with a sense of peace and light and direction. I have a strength I didn't know I had. Then, other times, I'm strong and sure, when I'm hit square between the eyes with the worst kind of pain. It still takes my breath away, and literally makes me feel like I'll throw up. It's been just over a month. It feels like so much longer.

When I was down in the worst places, I knew hope would break through. And when I was strong, I knew terrible pain would come.

Before Brian and I started going out, I had come to a place in life where I was content. It hadn't been easy—and the battle hadn't been completely won—but I was delighting in God as I never had before. Life was joyful, in spite of singleness. God's love filled my life.

I'm finding it hard to recover that contentment.

My natural, systemic worry is fueled by the gray hair that's becoming more noticeable and by an intense gnawing doubt that perhaps I'll never marry. I was designed to get married and have a family; it's built into my nature. I may never realize that dream. The potential loss is monumental. On my bad days, I don't know if I can live with that kind of disappointment and still keep my faith.

Is it possible to find victory here? It must be, with God's help.

If I'm not able to relinquish this dream, I'm afraid I'll be spiritually and emotionally crippled. God has to be able to get me past this.

At the same time, I feel rather foolish for feeling this pain so deeply. So many people out there have hurt much more than I have. I have a wonderful family and good friends; my needs are met more than abundantly.

Yet, I have the gall to be depressed about being single? It seems selfish and petty. God has given me so much—am I going to hold this against Him?

However small this issue may seem, for me it is a deeply personal and private pain. And the more single men and women I talk to, the more convinced I am that I'm not alone.

I hope this journey together leads us closer to wholeness, peace, and an intimate knowledge of God.

Chapter Two

YOU MAY NOT GET MARRIED

❧

"You know, Lori, the right guy is out there, and he's worth waiting for." Liz sipped her coffee and shot me a reassuring glance. As much as I love Liz, I couldn't believe her.

Liz was a "happy thinker." (After several single years, I had learned to fear them.) She was kind. She wanted me to be happy. She knew I wanted to be married. She thought God would give me what I wanted. She spoke with the assurance of the prophet in the wilderness. But what did she know?

Some send their warm wishes with a vengeance. They wear their marriage as a badge of honor that they have attained a level of spiritual maturity beyond us—they were completely content and waited on God without giving Him a timetable. They committed to being a long-term missionary in a small African village known for cannibalism. Whatever it was, they're sure if we would just do the same thing—attain the same spiritual maturity they had before they married—God would reward us. The worst of them chime, "Ah, well, God must have more to teach you."

At such well-meant idiocy (for it is idiotic, even though well-meant—can you imagine treating a cancer victim that way? "I'm so sorry the cancer spread to your liver; God must have more to teach you"), one question rises in the minds of the entire Christian single population: What in the world are they talking about? (And, ahem, just maybe...are they right?)

Here's the truth, as I see it: You and I may not get married—or remarried, as the case may be.

(We're getting the worst part over first.)

Call me a pessimist, a glass-half-empty girl, a little-faith. But I had to accept this truth before I could enjoy the single life God has given me, without always looking around the corner for what's coming next.

God promises to provide all our needs. He promises to be with us. He doesn't promise us a husband or wife. It has nothing to do with our spiritual maturity, and everything to do with God's plan for our lives.

I don't mean to imply that you shouldn't hope, but there's a wonderful freedom that comes when you face your worst fear head-on and—with God's grace—move beyond it.

Faulty Logic, Faulty Faith

Inevitably, people believe the most reassuring thing they can tell you is that it will all work out. God will bless you; the perfect husband or wife will come; you'll be married and have a beautiful family. They believe these blessings are nearly guaranteed for you. You're their friend, brother, daughter; they can't imagine your not getting married.

And it's easier for them—and for you—to believe that it will all work out. It's much harder to say, "Whatever happens, God will be with you; He knows what He's doing."

If we believe that God will bring us a husband or wife, we're only required to trust Him a little bit—enough to bring us that person. If we believe that no matter what, God will be in it, and will act on what is best both for us and for His eternal plan, then we have to trust God with all of our hearts. That's much harder.

This is just one example of the way our faith has gotten sloppy.

I recently overheard these comments:

"God is going to bless me; I know He is! I've been through so much lately—it's just been a time of fire, of trials, you know? So I know there's a huge blessing right around the corner."

"You know, if you do that, if you're faithful and give up Kyle—what's most important to you— you'll get a reward. If it's not getting him back, it's someone else. But it's something. God will reward you for that." (What about the reward of knowing God?)

We believe that having faith means believing that God has good things in store for us. We emphasize His goodness, kindness, love, and the tangible ways we *know* they'll work themselves out in our lives—a new job when we're suddenly laid off, a beautiful new house when we're forced to move, the perfect roommate, the health of a loved one, the perfect spouse. That's not faith.

Don't get me wrong. God does have good things in store for us, and He blesses us every day. It's not wrong to hope in that, and I'm not saying that in order to be a good Christian you have to hang your head and believe you're doomed. (Quite the opposite, in fact.)

We err when we use the logic, "Since God is good and desires to bless me, He will give me x." (Fill in the blank here—a wonderful husband, a new house, healing for a close friend.) We slip into a type of name-it-and-claim-it theology, believing that God will keep us from the things that would be most painful for us.

We say things like, "You'll get better soon; God is watching over you," implying that God heals those He watches over. What about the ones who die or remain sick? Did God forsake them?

Perhaps we do it because we don't want to face the truth about who God is; we sense there may be an uglier reality beneath all of this that we don't want to swallow.

It wouldn't take much effort to believe in a God who was always there pitching in at the right time with the perfect solution to each of our problems. The irony is, we know deep down inside that God—or life—doesn't really work that way, so it does take a great deal of effort to believe in this kind of fairy godmother God. We work and pray and trust, and the reality of faith and God eludes us.

When I interviewed Dr. Larry Crabb about his book, *Shattered Dreams*, he talked about our tendency to trust Christ for a good life:

> I was saved at age 8 at a boys' camp where the counselor had 80 boys look into a bonfire and said, "Boys, you have a choice to make. Trust Jesus or burn in the fires of hell forever." I thought that was a no-brainer so I trusted Jesus and I think when I trusted Him for salvation to go to heaven I think I was trusting Him for a good life. I think I was trusting Him for pleasant feelings, for nice circumstances, for everything going well: meeting a nice girl, marrying her, having wonderful kids, having great sex, having great money, having great health, all the blessings of life.
>
> And God has given me a ton of blessings—there's no question of that—but there have been some bumps. I had cancer four years ago—that wasn't part of the plan. My brother was killed in an airplane crash 11 years ago. My mother has Alzheimer's. As I got older I think I began to realize that God is not committed to the good that I thought He was committed to. One of my favorite quotes is from Oswald Chambers. He says, "The root of all sin is the suspicion that God is not good." I think I have always believed in His goodness but more on the basis of the way He would bless me than on the basis of His kindness and love.[1]

Genuine faith is believing that whatever decision God makes is the right one...and that He's still good. It's praying for a loved one and still believing in God when he or she dies anyway. It's trusting that God is good and His hand is at work even when there's a pain in your soul that goes beyond words.

God in "The Place of Excrement"

The Bible is full of stories about people for whom the call of faith meant tremendous difficulty. Abraham picked up his family and moved without any idea of where they would end up. Joseph was sold into slavery, spent years in a prison, and in the end, was wise enough to recognize that God meant it for good. For years, God's prophets were tortured and killed for speaking the truth. The hall of faith in Hebrews 11 honors those who "were killed by stoning, by being sawn in two; they were murdered by the sword. They went about with nothing but sheepskins or goatskins to cover them. They lost everything and yet were spurned and ill-treated by a world too evil to see their worth" (Heb. 11:37-38).

At this point, you may be thinking that you didn't really sign up for more than a camp bonfire and a simple decision between Jesus and hell, and you'd like to get out. Christianity isn't easy. The value in our pain is that through it God draws us to Himself, molds our clay into a better piece of work, and wears away rough edges around our heart.

This principle reverberates through Scripture, though perhaps no more clearly than in James:

> *Consider it pure joy, my brothers, whenever you face trials of many kinds, because you know that the testing of your faith develops perseverance. Perseverance must*

finish its work so that you may be mature and complete, not lacking anything (James 1:2-4 NIV).

J.B. Phillips translates the passage like this:

When all kinds of trials and temptations crowd into your lives, my brothers, don't resent them as intruders, but welcome them as friends! Realise that they come to test your faith and to produce in you the quality of endurance. But let the process go on until that endurance is fully developed, and you will find you have become men of mature character, men of integrity with no weak spots.

Paul repeats the theme again in Romans 5:

Since then it is by faith that we are justified, let us grasp the fact that we have peace with God through our Lord Jesus Christ. Through Him we have confidently entered into this new relationship of grace, and here we take our stand, in happy certainty of the glorious things He has for us in the future. This doesn't mean, of course, that we have only a hope of future joys—we can be full of joy here and now even in our trials and troubles. These very things will give us patient endurance; this in turn will develop a mature character, and a character of this sort produces a steady hope, a hope that will never disappoint us (Romans 5:1-5).

"Consider it pure joy...." I'm not anywhere near that. That's a verse I ignore whenever possible. Through the pain of my breakup with Brian, though, I got a few small glimpses into what it means to count it all joy.

At the beginning, God gave me hope through Pastor Blake's message that bleak Sunday morning. I had a vision of God taking my desperate feelings of grief, loneliness, and shame and using them to grow me into someone more like Himself. I was sustained by the hope that I would be changed and by the knowledge that God was close.

Several months later, on Easter Sunday, I sat in church thinking how ill-prepared I was for the Easter service, how little time I'd spent contemplating the sacrifice and miracle we celebrated. My closest friend, Jilian, was married on Good Friday. I'd moved the week before for the fifth time in as many years. I was exhausted. Then the choir sang, the Scripture was read, and I realized again the truth of the resurrection.

Nothing else mattered. God knew me. He had saved me. Jesus had risen. In the midst of darkness, God was a strong tower, the only place I was secure.

I was surprised—though I shouldn't have been—by these flashes of joy in the midst of what was for me the pit of despair. In many ways, God was closer in my deepest pain than He had been before.

Madeleine L'Engle, in *Two-Part Invention*, a biographical account of her marriage to Hugh Franklin, details their struggle with the cancer that eventually took Hugh's life. Madeleine talks about knowing God more intimately in "the place of excrement." She quotes these lines by Yeats, with the following commentary:

> But Love has pitched her mansion in
> The place of excrement;
> For nothing can be sole or whole
> That has not been rent....

…I hear different people tell of some good or lucky event and then say, "Surely the Lord was with me." And my hackles rise. My husband is desperately ill, so where is the Lord? What about that place of excrement? Isn't that where Love's mansion is pitched? Isn't that where God is?

Doesn't such an attitude trivialize the activities and concerns of the Maker? Doesn't it imply that God is with us only during the good and fortuitous times and withdraws or abandons us when things go wrong?

I will have nothing to do with a God who cares only occasionally. I need a God who is with us always, everywhere, in the deepest depths as well as the highest heights. It is when things go wrong, when the good things do not happen, when our prayers seem to have been lost, that God is most present. We do not need the sheltering wings when things go smoothly. We are closest to God in the darkness, stumbling along blindly.[2]

Genuine Faith: Hananiah, Mishael, and Azariah

One of my favorite stories is the one about Hananiah, Mishael, and Azariah. You may know them by the Babylonian names they were given after they went into captivity— Shadrach, Meshach, and Abednego. Trapped in a foreign land, under orders from the king to bow down or be burned alive, they responded with the utmost strength and grace:

> ..."O Nebuchadnezzar, we do not need to defend our-
> selves before you in this matter. If we are thrown into the
> blazing furnace, the God we serve is able to save us from
> it, and he will rescue us from your hand, O king. But
> even if he does not, we want you to know, O king, that we
> will not serve your gods or worship the image of gold you
> have set up" (Daniel 3:16-18).

"Our God can save us. He's strong enough to do that. But even if He doesn't—if He chooses not to—we refuse to bow. We love Him more than our own lives."

These men understood real faith.

They knew God's power: He was able to deliver them. They acknowledged His sovereignty: He could deliver them or not. The decision was completely His. They understood enough of God's faithfulness to know that He would deliver them one way or the other—by life or by death. They trusted implicitly that whatever choice God made was the right one; they knew God was good and made good choices. And they honored God's worthiness: Live or die, they would worship only Him.

Their obedience was not contingent on God's doing what they thought best or pleasant. They found the object of their affection in *God Himself*—not in what He could do for them.[3]

It seems audacious to compare the burden of singleness to a heroic leap into Nebuchadnezzar's furnace, but in at least one sense we're in the same predicament. We have to love God for God Himself, not for what He can do for us. He's powerful enough to answer our prayers, but He may choose not to. We love Him anyway. We love Him more than our own lives.

Fyodor Dostoyevsky, in *The Brothers Karamazov*, argues that the one-time complete sacrifice is sometimes easier than the smaller, ongoing sacrifices we are called to make. He's describing the faith of the youngest son, Alyosha, and his contemporaries, who were eager to play the martyr for a worthy cause.

> ...these youths do not understand that the sacrifice
> of one's life is in most cases the easiest of all sacri-
> fices, and that to sacrifice, for instance, five or six
> years of their life, full of youthful fervor, to hard
> and difficult study, if only to increase tenfold their
> powers of serving truth so as to be able to carry
> out the great work they have set their hearts on
> carrying out—that such a sacrifice is beyond the
> strength of many of them.[4]

Some of us are called to five or six years of "hard and difficult study," of finding contentment and serving Christ in a life we would not choose. Some of us are called to 10 or 20 years, or to a lifetime. And, in the end, our daily sacrifices add up to something very honorable.

God's Promises: Jeremiah 29:11

Jeremiah 29:11 hangs on my wall: " 'For I know the plans I have for you,' declares the Lord, 'plans to prosper you and not to harm you, plans to give you hope and a future.' " It's often frustrated me as another item in the "happy thinkers" arsenal. What does it mean? Does God have good plans for me, individually? What kind of good plans?

It's worthwhile to understand the history behind the promise, though if you've studied Old Testament history at all, the roles will be familiar:

- Judah (the southern kingdom of Israel): errant child; plays the harlot with her faith, looking for any other god than the one she already knows, even if it means sacrificing her own children.

- God: supreme Deity; loving father loathe to punish; sends a messenger to warn of punishment and call His children back.

- Nebuchadnezzar, King of Babylon: powerful aggressor sent to chastise (later becomes acquainted with Hananiah, Mishael, and Azariah, when he tries to get them to worship his image in Babylon).

- Jeremiah: prophet; in the middle of all the action, pulling out his hair for lack of an appreciative audience; must speak whatever God tells him to (Judah will be conquered if they do not repent) as often as God wants him to (over and over and over and over).

- False prophets: gain popularity by telling the people what they want to hear; claim to speak for God to give their message credibility (though I doubt they would make that claim in God's presence, since they're really just making everything up).

There were more gods than there were cities in Judah, including Baal, to whom they offered live sacrifices of Judean children. God equated their faithlessness to spiritual prostitution, and He said of them, "How skilled you are at pursuing love! Even the worst of women can learn from your ways" (Jer. 2:33). Yet, He pleaded with them to change. Jeremiah carried God's pleas to Judah for more than 20 years, until Jeremiah's heart was worn out.

Judah refused to change. Babylon attacked, as Jeremiah had prophesied. Nebuchadnezzar carried off all the men, women, and children who survived, along with the country's treasures. Second Chronicles sums up the situation:

The Lord, the God of their fathers, sent word to them through His messengers again and again, because He had pity on His people and on His dwelling place. But they mocked God's messengers, despised His words and scoffed at His prophets until the wrath of the Lord was aroused against His people and there was no remedy. He brought up against them the king of the Babylonians, who killed their young men with the sword in the sanctuary, and spared neither young man nor young woman, old man or aged. God handed all of them over to Nebuchadnezzar. He carried to Babylon all the articles from the temple of God, both large and small, and the treasures of the Lord's temple and the treasures of the king and his officials. They set fire to God's temple and broke down the wall of Jerusalem; they burned all the palaces and destroyed everything of value there. He carried into exile to Babylon the remnant, who escaped from the sword, and they became servants to him and his sons until the kingdom of Persia came to power (2 Chronicles 36:15-20).

The story didn't end with Judah's captivity. The people wanted hope. So false prophets proclaimed that Babylon would fall and that Judah would be packing up soon to head home. God had other plans, however; Judah's stay in Babylon would last 70 years.

To set things straight, Jeremiah (who was still in Judah) sent a letter to the exiles in Babylon telling them to relax and settle in a bit. In the midst of this letter sits the verse of 29:11, giving them, as a nation, the hope of a future in their own land with the God who continued to seek them:

> *This is what the Lord Almighty, the God of Israel, says to all those I carried into exile from Jerusalem to Babylon: "Build houses and settle down; plant gardens and eat what they produce. Marry and have sons and daughters; find wives for your sons and give your daughters in marriage, so that they too may have sons and daughters....Do not let the prophets and diviners among you deceive you. Do not listen to the dreams you encourage them to have. They are prophesying lies to you in My name. I have not sent them," declares the Lord. ..."When seventy years are completed for Babylon, I will come to you and fulfill My gracious promise to bring you back to this place.* **For I know the plans I have for you,"** *declares the Lord,* **"plans to prosper you and not to harm you, plans to give you hope and a future.** *Then you will call upon Me and come and pray to Me, and I will listen to you. You will seek Me and find Me when you seek Me with all your heart. I will be found by you,"*

declares the Lord, "and will bring you back from captivity. I will gather you from all the nations and places where I have banished you," declares the Lord, "and will bring you back to the place from which I carried you into exile" (Jeremiah 29:4-14).

Jeremiah 29:11 was given directly to the nation of Israel—not to each individual but to the nation as a whole. It was tied to their repentance and return to the Lord. At the end of 70 years, they would seek God with all their heart and find Him. He would then gather them back from all the places they were scattered. They'd have to wait much longer than their false prophets were predicting, but God hadn't given up on them. They did, in fact, have a future as a nation.

So what does this mean for each of us? The life of Jeremiah may be a telling example: Jeremiah was alone. No one liked him. His family and friends turned against him. His life was threatened more than once. He didn't enjoy being a prophet, but when he tried to keep quiet, he found that God's word was like "a fire shut up in [his] bones" (Jer. 20:9), and he couldn't keep from speaking it.

Kathleen Norris talks about Jeremiah's emotional highs and lows in *The Cloister Walk*:

The voice of Jeremiah is compelling, often on an overwhelmingly personal level. One morning, I was so worn out by the emotional roller coaster of chapter 20 that after prayers I walked to my apartment and went back to bed. This passionate soliloquy, which begins with a bitter outburst on the nature of the prophet's calling ("You enticed me, O

Lord, and I was enticed"), moves quickly into denial ("I say to myself, I will not mention him, I will speak his name no more. But then it becomes like fire burning in my heart, imprisoned in my bones"). Jeremiah's anger at the way his enemies deride him rears up, and also fear and sorrow ("All my close friends are watching for me to stumble"). His statement of confidence in God ("The Lord is with me like a dread warrior") seems forced under the circumstances, and a brief doxology ("Sing to the Lord, praise the Lord, for he has delivered the life of the needy from the hands of evildoers") feels more ironic than not, being followed by a bitter cry: "Cursed be the day that I was born." The chapter concludes with an anguished question: "Why did I come forth from the womb, to see sorrow and pain, to end my days in shame?"…

In the Book of Jeremiah we encounter a very human prophet, and a God who is alarmingly alive. Jeremiah makes it clear that no one chooses to fall into the hands of such a God. You are chosen, you resist, you resort to rage and bitterness and, finally, you succumb to the God who has given you your identity in the first place.[5]

God had good things planned for Judah, when they sought Him. He would continue to love them. He would forgive them. But part of that good plan was for Jeremiah to ceaselessly talk about it, even when no one would listen—a task that left Jeremiah with "a fire in his bones."

We singles share Jeremiah's predicament. We are chosen (though sometimes we see no grand purpose in the pain of our unfulfilled dreams), we resist God's choice for us, perhaps we resort to rage and bitterness, and eventually we give in. The beauty of Jeremiah 29:11 is that we know the nature of the God we are giving in to: He is forgiving. He doesn't give up easily. He wants us to seek Him; He wants to be found. On a grand scale, He is working out good plans that we have the privilege to be part of.

I'm still tempted to read the verse hanging on my wall and trivialize it—turn God into the fairy godmother who will show up with a beautiful gown and save me from scrubbing floors. But then I remember the man who wrote it—and the fire in my own bones—and I pray that, in the end, it will be a good part of a bigger plan.

God's Promises: Psalm 37:4

Psalm 37:4 is another difficult verse to understand. "Delight yourself in the Lord and He will give you the desires of your heart." The way we interpret it says a lot about our view of God. Is He cruel, in that He gives us desires only to watch us struggle when they go unfulfilled? One guy who e-mailed me thought so:

> To be satisfied without having a desire met. That is a tough thing to do. I think for God to give someone a desire to be married, which I believe is in His will for the majority of singles, and not meet that desire is cruel of God to do that.

31

Most of the interpretations I've heard for this verse say that rather than granting all your wishes, God will give you your desires—that is not grant them, but work with the actual substance of your desires so that your desires match His. But what do you do with the woman in her forties or fifties who still wants to be married, yet doesn't have any hope? For years she's begged God to take away this desire, but He hasn't.

Perhaps this verse should be interpreted to mean that God Himself will become the fulfillment of your desires. He will meet you; in knowing Him, the deepest desires of your soul will be met.

David's theme is that righteous people will be rewarded and evil people will be punished. The righteous don't have to worry about justifying themselves in men's eyes or punishing those who have wronged them. God will take care of all of this.

At the beginning of this Psalm, David exhorts us to righteousness, listing dozens of things we should do when we're wronged:

Do not fret because of evil men or be envious of those who do wrong; for like the grass they will soon wither, like green plants they will soon die away. Trust in the Lord and do good; dwell in the land and enjoy safe pasture. Delight yourself in the Lord and He will give you the desires of your heart. Commit your way to the Lord; trust in Him and He will do this: He will make your righteousness shine like the dawn, the justice of your cause like the noonday sun. Be still before the Lord and wait patiently for Him; do not fret when men succeed in their ways, when they carry out their wicked schemes. Refrain from anger and turn from wrath; do not fret—it leads only to evil. For evil men will be cut off, but those who hope in the Lord will inherit the land (Psalm 37:1-9).

We often focus entirely on verse 4 and neglect the other commands this passage contains:

- do not fret or be envious
- trust in the Lord
- do good
- dwell in the land
- enjoy safe pasture
- delight yourself in the Lord
- commit your way to the Lord
- trust in Him
- be still before the Lord
- wait patiently for Him
- do not fret
- refrain from anger
- turn from wrath
- DO NOT FRET! (emphasis mine).

David emphasizes the fact that God is faithful to the righteous. He will defend their cause and protect their justice. We know that if He doesn't defend us now, He will in the end. We have nothing to fear. Ultimately, we will be saved.

When we delight in God, our perspective on life changes—part of the radical transformation described in Romans 12. "Don't let the world around you squeeze you into its own mould, but let God re-make you so that your whole attitude of mind is changed. Thus you will prove in practice that the will of God is good, acceptable to Him, and perfect" (Rom. 12:2). Rather than focusing on what our desires are and how God is meeting them or not meeting them, or changing them or not changing them, we need to delight, to rest, to trust.

I struggle with believing that God wants me to delight in Him. In a journal entry last March, I wrote:

God wants us to dance at His feet, to delight in Him.

I cower at God's feet. I don't dance.

But there's so much to cower from, and so many reasons to hide. Even if I've confessed everything that I can think of, there's so much that's just evil inside me—so much of the core of who I am—that I just can't confess it all.

So I hide, I sheepishly step forward and give my too-short prayers. (If guilt keeps me from praying, it also haunts me when I pray—surely they are not in the right format, long enough, sincere enough—and exactly why am I not getting up at 4 a.m. to pray? I have no good excuses. The history of the saints is enough to condemn me.)

Maybe you've felt the same way. I wish I could delight in God without any second thoughts. I hope He will teach me how to do that.

I still don't understand exactly how to apply Psalm 37:4 to my life. I think, though, that the main point of the verse is that delighting in God is the key to handling our desires. The delighting should be our focus; the desires, God's. We also need to remember the other commands, which are equally as important: don't worry, trust God, do good, and stay away from anger.

JUMPING OFF THE CLIFF

My friend Sarah put it like this:

I'm having a really hard time with God right now. I feel like I'm standing at the top of a cliff, and being told to jump. And everyone says that God will catch me, but He doesn't always catch you. And faith means that you have to jump anyway. How do you live with that?

So many people act like it doesn't happen—you won't get hurt if you're a Christian. But you do. Sometimes you do. Don't people think? I mean, there were Christians in the holocaust who were killed—young women and children. Didn't God care about them? It doesn't always work out.

The truth that we as singles have to face is that we may not get married. For me—and maybe for you—facing that is like jumping off a cliff without anyone to catch me. I have to accept this possibility and believe that God is still good, no matter what.

Chapter Three

You're Right Where God Wants You to Be

❧

One of the worst things about being single is the self-doubt. Somehow you can't escape from wondering if your predicament is somehow your own fault—and friends or family are likely to speculate about what your problem is and offer their suggestions. Perhaps you need to find a church with more single people. Maybe you just need to be more social. Maybe you're too independent and need to work on sending the right "I'm-available-and-looking-for-you!" vibes. And why exactly did you break up with that person you were dating last year? Huh. Too bad. They were so nice.

I've been overwhelmed lately with regrets from my college days. I cringe when I think of things I longed to do but didn't have the courage to try, or was too proud to fail, to admit that I had more to learn, to be willing to be taught. I look back and see failure, for there was some of that. But I wonder at the cause for my search. I search because I sense that I *have* failed, that my single 30-something life is proof in itself that my life went wrong somewhere. Perhaps this was not God's original, good plan for my life. Perhaps my strong nature and pride were constantly twisting my life events beyond God's ability or desire to reach down and put them right.

God's will is a complicated topic. God is not understandable—I can approach Him, depend on Him, feel that I know Him, but I cannot understand Him. And I can't understand the way He works in our lives. He controls everything and longs for a certain outcome, yet He's given us all free choice. Can I ruin His plans for my life by choosing the wrong things? Have I done that?

The Mysterious Guide

God leads us. We know this is true. There are disagreements as to exactly how He leads us, but there's a long, beautiful history of His leading.

He spoke to Samuel with a loud voice at night. With Mary and Joseph, He used angels. Balaam's donkey actually spoke to him. God used three days in the whale to change Jonah's heart. Israel followed a cloud by day and a pillar of fire by night. The Holy Spirit told the church leaders in Antioch to set Barnabas and Saul aside for a special work He had called them to do.

The Bible presents a clear picture of God's guiding us: Jesus is our light and salvation; the Bible is a lamp to our feet and a light to our path; God is our guide; the Spirit leads us into all truth. The Bible also presents a very real God who is close to us, knows our every step, and directs us. If you're walking with God, then He's with you, and He can and will direct you.

Psalm 23 presents God as our shepherd and guide, both in the calm places of life (the green pastures and quiet waters) and in the most difficult things we face (the valley of the shadow of death). He is always with us, and He comforts us.

Psalm 139 presents a God whose knowledge of us is so intimate that He knows when we eat, when we lie down, and what we're going to say before we say it. He wove us together before we were born; He knows all the days that are planned for us. Verses 5-10 speak specifically to His guidance:

You hem me in—behind and before; You have laid Your hand upon me. Such knowledge is too wonderful for me, too lofty for me to attain. Where can I go from Your Spirit? Where can I flee from Your presence? If I go up to the heavens, You are there; if I make my bed in the depths, You are there. If I rise on the wings of the dawn, if I settle on the far side of the sea, even there Your hand will guide me, Your right hand will hold me fast.

God holds us. He surrounds us. He guides us.

Psalm 25 reveals God's guidance into holiness and away from sin:

Good and upright is the Lord; therefore He instructs sinners in His ways. He guides the humble in what is right and teaches them His way....Who, then, is the man that fears the Lord? He will instruct him in the way chosen for him (Psalm 25:8-9, 12).

Psalm 32 is the well-known psalm David wrote after he had confessed his sin of adultery to God. After David praises the blessings of God's forgiveness, God speaks:

I will instruct you and teach you in the way you should go; I will counsel you and watch over you. Do not be like the horse or the mule, which have no understanding but must be controlled by bit and bridle or they will not come to you (Psalm 32:8-9).

CHRIST, OUR AIM

God's promise to guide us is often directly related to His desire to mold our character. The Bible picture is not necessarily that of a boss giving us our next set of orders, but of a companion who shows us how to live. The Scriptures that discuss God's leading often refer to His promises to guide us in His way and His truth—something that's not so tangible as "Should I stay here or move to Seattle?" but that gets more to the core of who we are. This is true both of the Old Testament references we've looked at and of Paul's instruction in the New Testament. He writes to the Thessalonians, "It is God's will that you should be sanctified" (1 Thess. 4:3 NIV), and again, "give thanks in all circumstances, for this is God's will for you in Christ Jesus" (1 Thess. 5:18 NIV).

Elisabeth Elliot, in her book *God's Guidance: A Slow and Certain Light*, says that we often come to God in search of a simple answer, when what we really need is God Himself:

We know what we need—a yes or no answer,
please, to a simple question. Or perhaps a road
sign. Something quick and easy to point the way.
What we really ought to have is the Guide himself.[6]

And that is just what God is trying to give us—Himself, and us more in His image. For Elisabeth, "Christ, in other words, is the ultimate objective. Christ himself is also the way."[7] She quotes a prayer by Phillips Brooks that recognizes the value of this end:

> O Lord, by all thy dealings with us, whether of joy or pain, of light or darkness, let us be brought to thee. Let us value no treatment of thy grace simply because it makes us happy or because it makes us sad, because it gives us or denies us what we want; but may all that thou sendest us bring us to thee...[8]

It's a sentiment that Paul echoes in Phillipians: "...I look upon everything as loss compared with the overwhelming gain of knowing Christ Jesus my Lord" (3:8).

THE ART OF FOLLOWING

It seems that if only God would make His will a little bit clearer, we would be glad to follow, but it can be so hard to discern. You may feel led in one direction, but how clear is that leading? How sure are you? We long for certainty, and God's path for our lives is often murky, at best. There is a scene in *The Fellowship of the Ring* when the company is in the mines of Moria, the ancient dwarf world of Khazad-dum, trying to find their way under the mountains. Gandalf, their leader, stops for a time in front of three doors, leading to three different tunnels. The success of their journey hinges upon his choosing the right way, but he's stumped. He finally chooses the tunnel that smells best. Our choices seem to be just as random at times.

Thomas Merton captured the angst of struggling to know God's will, wanting to please Him, and having faith when He seems to be distant:

My Lord God, I have no idea where I am going.

I do not see the road ahead of me. I cannot know
for certain where it will end. Nor do I really know
myself, and the fact that I think I am following
Your will does not mean that I am actually doing
so. But I believe that the desire to please You does
in fact please You. And I hope I have that desire in
all that I am doing. I hope that I will never do anything apart from that desire. And I know that, if I
do this, You will lead me by the right road, though
I may know nothing about it. Therefore I will trust
You always though I may seem to be lost and in
the shadow of death. I will not fear, for You are
ever with me, and You will never leave me to face
my perils alone.[9]

The preponderance of biblical evidence suggests that we should not worry at all about whether or not we've correctly discerned God's will for our lives. The whole idea that you could miss God's plan by buying the wrong house or choosing the wrong job is completely missing from the Bible. You never see Paul or Daniel or Joseph or Ruth worrying about missing God's will, and they were all thrown into situations that might make them wonder. Paul was shipwrecked, tortured, and stoned. Daniel was taken into captivity and thrown into the lions' den. Joseph's brothers sold him into slavery; then he was wrongly accused of rape and thrown into prison. Ruth's husband died, and she became an exile in a strange country.

God is most concerned that we love Him, that we follow Him in obedience. He is fully capable of reaching down at any time in our lives and moving us wherever we need to be to accomplish His will. He sent an angel to tell Philip where to go to meet the Ethiopian eunuch, then mysteriously took Philip away when that task was completed. He directed Paul both through dreams and through his various arrests and imprisonments. But this divine direction is always His to worry about—never ours.

Garry Friesen, in his book *Decision Making and the Will of God*, goes so far as to suggest that God does not have a specific individual will for each of our lives, as many churches have traditionally taught. Much of our angst about following God comes from this teaching about an individual will—a plan that encompasses where we should go to college, whom or if we should marry, where we should work, where we should worship. Many of us were taught to diligently seek the will of God in these areas of our lives, with the implied warning that if we made the wrong choices, we may forego God's best for our lives—and may not be able to get back. Following God becomes not only a question of loving Him and humbly submitting in obedience, but also one of discerning His specific will for our individual life situations, which cannot be gleaned from the Bible but must be sought through an innate sense of His desires, the advice of friends and family, and inner peace. Friesen describes this as a misinterpretation of biblical teaching, which often leads to frustration because this individual will for each of our lives can be nearly impossible to discern:

> I have met many believers who were frustrated because they were convinced that God loved them

and had a wonderful plan for their lives, but for
some reason He was not telling them what it was.
Are Christians like so many laboratory rats, con-
signed to explore every dead end in the maze of
life, while the One who knows the way through
just watches?[10]

If you can't find that specific individual will, you feel guilty—
God no doubt is doing His part, but you're failing to understand the signals He sends.

Friesen believes that each biblical reference to God's will
for our lives can be interpreted as referring to His moral will
("God's moral commands" that teach us how to live) or to His
sovereign will ("God's predetermined plan for everything
that happens in the universe"[11]). Friesen concludes that God
does guide us, specifically through all the teaching He's given
us in the Bible, the instruction in right living and the way of
wisdom. God leaves individual decisions to us, requiring
only that we make wise decisions and stay within the moral
boundaries He's established. And the best way to please
God? It's not by guessing the correct answers to a series of life
questions; it's by obeying Him.

Is your greatest goal in life to please the heart of
God? If you are His child through faith in Jesus
Christ, the process is clear: Learn, love, and obey
the moral will of God.[12]

Friesen's fresh perspective on this is valuable. It's possible we've placed too much emphasis on the concept of an
individual will. But there are still examples of this individual
will in Scripture—Jeremiah and John the Baptist, who were

set apart from birth for a special calling; David, who became an unlikely choice to be king in his teens; and the many times the apostles prayed for God's direction in their activities. Then there are our own lives. Although I haven't been able to discern a detailed, step-by-step plan, there have been times of clarity, times when I knew that, regardless of anything else, I had to move forward into the task God had prepared for me.

Blaine Smith, best-selling author of *Knowing God's Will*, balances Friesen's approach. He points out that though God does have a specific will for our lives, He doesn't always tell us clearly what that will is, and He often requires that we get involved in the process by diligently seeking and using the wisdom and reason He's given us:

> It is through our normal, rational decision process-
> es that we discover God's leading, provided that
> we approach our decision making with a heart
> toward doing God's will....While God can, if he
> chooses, lead us contrary to reason, we may trust
> that in such cases he will make his directions
> unmistakeably clear. Apart from such dramatic
> guidance, our responsibility is to make as sound a
> decision as possible, trusting that he in his provi-
> dence will give us all the information we need to
> decide within his will.[13]

God is guiding us through the events of our lives, the information and opportunities He gives us, and the wisdom that we gradually become more adept at discerning. It's clear that we do not need to worry about whether or not we've missed God's plan—it seems it's not possible to truly seek

God and make the wrong decision. If you've sought to follow God, you can be confident you're where He wants you to be.

AND IF NOT GOD

I will never forget Claire. I met her at my first singles' retreat, and by the lunch break on the first day she was in the bathroom sobbing. She poured out her story: "I just don't know what to do. How can God do anything with my life? I've completely messed up. I've been divorced—not just once, but twice. And the second time, I knew what I was doing. And my son looks at me and knows—he knows I messed up, that I didn't live the way I taught him to. How in the world can God do anything with my life now? I'm beyond hope. I've messed everything up."

Some of us are single because we've made mistakes—we married too young, married the wrong person, married an unbeliever, had an affair, walked out on a spouse, or watched someone walk out on us. How could this be God's will for us? Is His will completely lost? Is it possible to be used of God, to be favored, when you know that you're the one responsible for your mess?

I was talking to my good friend April about my own failures, and hers, and we agreed that God specializes in using poor raw material in order to show what good work He does. She said, "There's a whole litany of horrible people that God used in mighty, mighty ways." Most of the Bible's key characters have serious faults. Rahab was a prostitute. Ruth was a Moabitess—a Gentile whom the Jews were forbidden to marry. And yet, both Rahab and Ruth were in the ancestral line of Christ. David, the "man after God's own heart," was a horrible father, an adulterer, a murderer. Jacob had a well-deserved reputation as a liar. And Esther most likely slept her way into her queenly role in a competition that was a bit more risqué than the average beauty contest.

God isn't crippled by our mistakes. In spite of ourselves, in spite of what other people have done and will do to us, God will do something good with us and in us. He forgives us completely. His grace is abundant and free. And He specializes in bringing good things out of bad situations. Paul—who was an authority on the topic, having had what looks from the outside like a streak of amazing bad luck and having a history as one of the early Church's fiercest attackers—tells us that whatever happens, God will bring good out of it when we're following Him: "Moreover we know that to those who love God, who are called according to His plan, everything that happens fits into a pattern for good" (Rom. 8:28).

Sometimes we sin and face the results. And though these results may linger, God always forgives. Sometimes we bear the brunt of someone else's sin, and God mysteriously uses even our pain for the sake of something good.

TODAY'S GIFT

Since we know that God is at work in our lives, I believe it's possible to view our present circumstances as His gift to us, for today. Most singles cringe when the "gift of singleness" comes up, afraid that perhaps they've been chosen for a lifetime sacrifice they never requested. One woman wrote, "I'm afraid if I make any attempt to accept my singleness God will see that as an 'okay' sign that I want to be single the rest of my life." Elisabeth Elliot argues that singleness, for however long we have it, is in fact a gift:

> If you are single today, the portion assigned to you for today is singleness. It is God's gift. Singleness ought not to be viewed as a problem, nor marriage as a right. God in His wisdom and love grants either as a gift. An unmarried person has the gift of singleness, not to be confused with the gift of celibacy. When we speak of the "gift of celibacy," we usually refer to one who is bound by vows not to marry. If you are not so bound, what may be your portion tomorrow is not your business today. Today's business is trust in the living God who precisely measures out, day by day, each one's portion.[14]

Albert Hsu, in *Singles at the Crossroads*, stresses that both marriage and singleness are gifts from God:

> *If you are single, then you have the gift of singleness.* If you are married, you don't. If you marry, you exchange the gift of singleness for the gift of marriedness. Both are good. Simple as that.[15]

Hsu also quotes John Stott, the British theologian and elder statesmen who has been single for all of his 70-plus years. Stott explains that his call to singleness came about gradually as he sought God's will day by day, year by year. He did not know at 20 that he would always be single. Stott believes that this is generally the way God works when calling us to singleness:

> I personally believe...that people discover it gradually and as the years pass begin to think that God

is not calling them to marry. They don't meet a
person with whom they believe God is calling
them to share their life, or they don't fall deeply in
love, or their work develops in such a way that it
seems right for them to remain single in order to
give themselves to their work rather than to a family. And as circumstances build up in this way,
they begin to discern that God is calling them to be
single. And that is more the situation with me.[16]

Stott encourages us,

...be patient. Pray daily that God will guide you to
your life partner or show you if he wants you to
remain single. Second, lead a normal social life.
Develop many friendships. Third, if God calls you
to singleness, don't fight it.[17]

It's not necessarily true that God wants you to be single
forever simply because you're single today. It's not wrong to
seek to be married, to pray for marriage. The challenge is to
trust God when His decisions and directions in this area don't
make sense to us. Elisabeth Elliot notes that trust is central to
our requests for guidance:

Our prayers for guidance (or anything else) really
begin here: I trust him. This requires abandonment. We are no longer saying, "If I trust him, he'll
give me such and such," but, "I trust him. Let him
give me or withhold from me what he chooses."[18]

GOD BLESSES YOU HERE

Dear friend, not only are you where you're supposed to be, but you're blessed. As singles, we often look at the blessing that's been denied us and fail to see beyond that. I could tally the benefits of singleness—absolute control over the TV remote, the ability to spend your money however you want, the freedom to get wrapped up in a novel until 3 a.m., and a social calendar that includes meeting friends at Starbucks without whiny children in tow. But I think the novelty of those things wears off, and there's much better stuff below the surface. The God who led you here blesses you with His presence and with the knowledge of Him. God is near to you; He understands you; He teaches you; He sustains your soul; He washes you thoroughly from your sin; He takes account of your tears; He is a stronghold, a help; you can hide in the shadow of His wings; He is a strong refuge; He is the strength of your heart; He is abundant in love, ready to forgive; you can trust Him with all your heart; He is gracious and compassionate; you can rest in Him; He is a strong fortress; He helps you; He is faithful.

In addition to His presence, there are so many other things to be thankful for. Singer/songwriter Bebo Norman, in an article for ChristianityToday.com's Singles Channel, said:

> The truth is, I'm single because I'm single. That's
> the hand I've been dealt. And you know what? It's
> not a bad hand. I think the trick to life is just to be
> thankful. In all things, be thankful.[19]

The skeptic in me still finds it hard to say with certainty that you or I are right where we're supposed to be, in the place God had planned for us. But I believe this is true. I believe that God is at work behind the scenes in ways we don't understand. And I think that this issue—whether or not we are single or married—pales in comparison to His overriding goal for our lives, which is to make us like Him, to draw us to Him. We may still find ourselves praying along with Thomas Merton, "I have no idea where I am going." And I think that's all right.

Chapter Four

You Have No Need to Be Ashamed

❧

"Jennifer, it's normal to get married." Jennifer sat in the middle of the minivan, surrounded by nieces and nephews, on the way home from her thirtieth-birthday family lunch. Her brother, 15 years older, became a Christian at 15, married at 20, had five kids, a stay-at-home wife, and annual summer trips to the same little beach bungalow with the outdoor shower, the family dog, and hours smothering suntan lotion on wet kids with bathing suits full of sand. By his definition, Jennifer was abnormal—single, 30, career, no kids, no boyfriend. Not that she wasn't trying, but the last few boyfriends hadn't been winners. One expected sexual favors. One had no sense of humor. One was ready to marry her two weeks after they met. Jennifer was devastated by her brother's comment: "What is he thinking? That I'm not trying? That I'm too picky? That I should just take whoever comes along? I just started to cry."

There seems to be a caste system at work in the Church— or perhaps not so much a caste system as a general order of life, a series of steps you must take in order to be "all grown up": college, marriage, baby, kids. Those of us who fail to complete all the steps or who stick a divorce in there somewhere feel as though we may have failed at what was perhaps our highest calling. Perhaps we have less to give God because we aren't married (as some churches infer by limiting leadership roles to those who have spouses). Perhaps we aren't quite as valuable as our married friends. As Albert Hsu wrote in *Singles at the Crossroads*, "In circles where marriage seems to be the rite of passage into adulthood, singles are perceived as developmentally challenged."[20]

This perception isn't limited to the Church. *Bridget Jones's Diary* captured the plight of "Singletons" everywhere:

> "So," bellowed Cosmo, pouring me a drink. "How's your love life?"
>
> Oh no. Why do they do this? Why? Maybe the Smug Marrieds only mix with other Smug Marrieds and don't know how to relate to individuals anymore. Maybe they really do want to patronize us and make us feel like failed human beings....
>
> "Yes, why aren't you married yet, Bridget?" sneered Woney...with a thin veneer of concern whilst stroking her pregnant stomach.
>
> ...I merely simpered apologetically, at which point someone called Alex piped up, "Well, you know, once you get past a certain age..."

"Exactly...All the decent chaps have been snapped
up," said Cosmo, slapping his fat stomach and
smirking so that his jowls wobbled.[21]

Many of us have spent hours crafting imaginary rants in
reponse to insolent questions, as do Bridget's friends:

"You should have said 'I'm not married because
I'm a Singleton, you smug, prematurely aging, nar-
rowminded morons,' " Shazzer ranted. " 'And
because there's more than one...way to live: one in
four households are single, most of the royal family are single, the nation's young men have been
proved by surveys to be completely unmarriage-
able, and as a result there's a whole generation of
single girls like me with their own incomes and
homes who have lots of fun and don't need to
wash anyone else's socks. We'd be as happy as
larks if people like you didn't conspire to make us
feel stupid just because you're jealous.' "[22]

Although women seem to carry the heaviest burden in
this regard—a bachelor has always held more social cachet
than an "old maid"—guys aren't exempt from feeling out of
place. One guy wrote the following to me:

The loneliness does get to be oppressive sometimes. Something that comforts me in my own
warped world is knowing—not understanding, but
knowing—there are so many people like us going
through the same thing. I guess there's safety in
numbers. I'm not such a freak, perhaps.

Perhaps that's what we're all hoping for—some kind of justification of our situation, affirmation that though the world around us is married, it's okay for us to be single. That we're not such freaks after all.

There are so many things in the Church that conspire against us. The belief that marriage is normal—not necessarily a problem in itself—is often accompanied by the corollary "singleness is abnormal," as Jennifer's brother determined. One single woman in her forties wrote to me:

> I even had one [Christian woman] ask me if I was
> a lesbian because "all the straight women are mar-
> ried." There are times when I have felt like I
> should have a tin cup when I walk into my church.
> I feel like I should announce my presence like the
> lepers in the Bible, "Unclean! Single! Unclean!"

Nurseries, kids, Pioneer Girls, AWANA, vacation Bible school, sweetheart banquets, marriage classes, youth groups, engagements, weddings, babies. These are normal. It is not normal to be alone. And it is perhaps sinful to be divorced. Now, all of these things may be true, in some situations. Divorce is a symptom of a broken world, often caused by the willful selfishness of one person. And when you think about it, the typical pattern is to grow up, get married (though marriages are happening later in life than they used to), and have a family. It's what we all expected—and it may still happen. The problem is that when you're sitting in the pew, all of the church's emphasis on the family seems to scream out at you: "It's *normal* to get married! And you aren't either— married or normal."

This philosophy is so prevalent that it's possible to soak it up without realizing it, as though it's been seeping in through your left ear while your right was busy listening to the sermon. You may think you're doing okay, but underneath all those layers of thought there's a dissatisfaction with your life, with yourself, a feeling that you don't measure up somehow. A feeling that you should be married by now, and perhaps your mother's disappointment is justified.

It can make you feel like Freddie, the kid who was held back in third grade. It wasn't his fault that he was bad at math or that his mom worked the night shift and couldn't help him with compound fractions. But he was branded; he didn't fit with the fourth graders anymore, or with the up-coming third graders. There was really no place for him. He would always be stuck in between, as are we—stuck between the "appropriate" college-era single and the "normal" married world.

All of that can make you wonder: Why? What is so hideous about me that I have not been chosen, that I have been rejected, unable to meet a suitable match? Shouldn't three or four decades be enough? And if it's not something physical or emotional, the predominant theory is that it may be spiritual. Katie ran into an old boyfriend and his new wife at church. They asked if she was seeing anyone—she wasn't—and told her, "Well, God must still have something to teach you." That sentiment is rarely voiced, but many Christians assume that if you're single, you're somehow not spiritual enough to marry. And many singles believe it.

A LITTLE HISTORY

Albert Hsu, in *Singles at the Crossroads*, presents a history of singleness within the Church. He begins with Jewish culture, in which family was central to community life:

> The Old Testament Israelite community, like most of the ancient world, was based on family clans and stressed the importance of marriage and children. "The Old Testament provides no real place for single people," Rodney Clapp writes. "Even ascetics such as priests and Nazirites were not single (Lev 21:1-15; Num 6:1-21). In fact, for a Hebrew not getting married was catastrophic." To be without spouse and children was to be without inheritors and guardians in old age. In Jewish society, marriage was the norm. Children were seen as blessings and were expected of every married couple.[23]

K.C. Hanson and Douglas Oakman, in *Palestine at the Time of Jesus*, point out that the Talmud sets 18 as the appropriate age for a man to marry.[24] Presumably, women married younger than men. Hsu explains that one reason family was so important was that the Jews had only a vague understanding of eternal life and thus looked to children to offer some kind of immortality. Thus, the women who struggled with infertility—Sarah, Rachel, Hannah—were looked upon as insufficient, neglected by God.

And into this cultural environment, enter Jesus:

> Jesus came into this Jewish culture and shattered all their prejudices. In sharp contrast to Jewish conventional wisdom, Jesus taught that salvation

is not found in marriage and that eternal life does
not come from having sons to carry the family
name....Dignity and personhood come not from
marriage and progeny but from identity within the
kingdom of God.[25]

Jesus taught that marriage was not an eternal state,
established the Church as a new kind of family ("...with a
gesture of His hand towards His disciples He went on, 'There
are My mother and brothers! For whoever does the will of My
Heavenly Father is brother and sister and mother to Me' "
[Mt. 12:48-49]), and taught that allegiance to Christ and the
Church should take precedence over familial ties. This new
allegiance had the potential to cause division in the closest
family relationships ("For I have come to set a man against
his own father, a daughter against her own mother, and a
daughter-in-law against her mother-in-law" [Mt. 10:35]).[26]

There was divorce during Jesus' day, though just how
much is difficult to determine. Hanson and Oakman conclude that "the rabbinic school of Hillel...seems to represent
the dominant Israelite practice of allowing a man to divorce
his wife for any displeasure with her...."[27] So we can assume
that there were some who were single because of divorce.
However, in that patriarchal society where men were the *de
facto* head of the household, a single daughter or sister would
have, at any age, been dependent upon her father or brother.
The model of the single, independent woman probably did
not exist. Although it was possible under some circumstances for a woman to obtain a divorce, it was rare and was
seen as shameful.

People occasionally say, in support of singleness, "Well, Jesus was single, you know." And I wonder what in the world that has to do with my life. Jesus—more than any of the rest of us—had a divine call on His life; He was divine, in fact. It seems almost natural for Him to be single. If anyone could handle it, He could. But He wasn't single in a world like ours, where, as out of place as we feel at times, nearly half of the adult population is single. He was single in a world in which everyone was expected to marry. Perhaps His singleness was more than just a fact about His life, as it is for you or me. Perhaps it was a statement about life and about the value of one person aside from any marriage relationship.

The next great single Christian leader was Paul, who praised the value of singleness and wished that more people could be single, as he was. This was as countercultural to the early Church as it was to the Jews:

> In the early church, singleness was viewed as a truly freeing and liberating opportunity. A young Christian in the second century would have heard an onslaught of family-values rhetoric—coming not from the Christian community but from pagan sources. In ancient Greco-Roman culture, marriage and procreation were seen as civic duties. All good citizens were pressured to be productive members of society, in the literal sense of providing many offspring who would become craftsmen and soldiers to fill roles necessary for the functioning of civilized society. Furthermore, arranged marriages were still common. Children were expected to marry well and continue the family's name and prestige.[28]

So we find that Christianity came to two cultures—Jewish and Greco-Roman—in which family played too prominent a role, and Christianity offered a freeing alternative: singleness. Hsu concludes: "Compared to the Jewish attitudes of the first century, Jesus and Paul were truly revolutionary. Their very lives as single adults provided role models for Christians who may have never seen an unmarried religious leader before."[29]

THE FOUR EUNUCHS OF THE APOCALYPSE

The Bible doesn't say much about singleness, and what it does say can be obscure and difficult to understand. First, there is Jesus talking to the disciples in Matthew 19. The Pharisees question Jesus about marriage and divorce, and Jesus tells them, "...anyone who divorces his wife on any grounds except her unfaithfulness and marries some other woman commits adultery" (Mt. 19:9). The disciples were astonished. In their words, "If that is a man's position with his wife, it is not worth getting married!" (Mt. 19:10)

Christ responds that not every man can accept this truth and stay single—"only those who have a special gift" as Phillips translates it, or "those to whom it has been given" in the New International Version. He speaks of eunuchs, who were common in those days in various important government positions. Castrated, and thus deemed more trustworthy, they were employed to watch the king's harem or the king's finances, and some may have mutilated themselves in hopes that this would make them of better service to the Kingdom of Heaven. A literal reading of the passage makes it seem that Jesus is perhaps encouraging self-mutilation, although He adds the qualification that it is for those men who "can accept [it]," which makes you think that would certainly limit the pool:

> *It is not everybody who can accept this principle,"* replied
> Jesus, *"only those who have a special gift. For some are*
> *incapable of marriage from birth, some are made inca-*
> *pable by the action of men, and some have made them-*
> *selves so for the sake of the kingdom of Heaven. Let the*
> *man who can accept what I have said accept it* (Matthew
> 19:11-12).

Another possible translation is that of the New International Version, "For some are eunuchs because they were born that way; others were made that way by men; and others have renounced marriage because of the kingdom of heaven. The one who can accept this should accept it" (Mt. 19:12).

Castration was hardly a cornerstone of Jesus's teaching about the Kingdom, and its relation to this passage is confusing, at best. What's clear, though, according to Jesus, is that singleness provides unique value to God's work, and that, if possible, we should welcome this opportunity. As Hsu points out, this message would have been radical to the Jewish audience who saw marriage as a prerequisite to spiritual value:

> ...the significance of Jesus' teaching in Matthew 19
> is that it affirms that *single persons are no less whole*
> *people for lack of marriage,* in contrast to Jewish
> thought. Rather, both married and unmarried peo-
> ple are equally able to serve God. Those who have
> "renounced marriage because of the kingdom"
> (v. 12 NIV) are honored as complete individuals

who have chosen a life of selfless service and
devotion to Christ their King.[30]

Paul's lengthy chapter on singleness and marriage in
First Corinthians begins with an endorsement of singleness:
"It is good for a man not to marry" (1 Cor. 7:1 NIV). Then the
next verse immediately switches tracks: "But since there is so
much immorality, each man should have his own wife, and
each woman her own husband" (NIV). The two parallel
themes run throughout the chapter—singleness is good ("Yet
to those who are unmarried or widowed, I say definitely that
it is a good thing to remain unattached, as I am," v. 8), but not
at the expense of purity ("But if they cannot control themselves, they should marry, for it is better to marry than to
burn with passion" [v. 9 NIV]). Paul actually thought that the
people he was writing to might be *happier* if they remained
single. He says of the widow, "she is free to marry whom she
likes—but let her be guided by the Lord. In my opinion she
would be happier to remain as she is, unmarried. And I think
I am here expressing not only my opinion, but the will of the
Spirit as well" (vv. 39-40).

Paul urges his audience to be content where they are,
not to put too much energy into getting out of their current
situation—whatever that is: "I merely add to the above that
each man should live his life with the gifts that the Lord has
given him and in the condition in which God has called
him....My brothers, let every one of us continue to live his life
with God in the state in which he was when he was called"
(vv. 17, 24). *The Message* translates verse 17 this way: "...don't
be wishing you were someplace else or with someone else.
Where you are right now is God's place for you. Live and
obey and love and believe right there. God, not your marital

status, defines your life."[31] Garry Friesen, in *Decision Making and the Will of God*, expounds on these verses:

> In I Corinthians 7:17-24, Paul sets forth an overriding principle that applies to all Christians regardless of their state. To the married, the single, the divorced, the widowed, the circumcised, the uncircumcised, the enslaved, the free, Paul says: 'Brethren, let each man remain with God in the condition in which he was called' (I Corinthians 7:24). Make it the goal of your life not to change your status, but to serve God as effectively and energetically as possible in whatever state you are....
>
> In declaring this principle Paul was not forbidding marriage for single people or freedom for slaves. If the opportunity comes along and it is expedient to take it, do so (7:21). His point was that people tend to concentrate on the wrong things. They pour their energies into changing their condition for their own sake rather than into changing the world for Christ's sake.[32]

As Christ did, Paul stresses the value of singleness in providing the opportunity to be single-hearted in devotion to the faith:

> *The unmarried man is free to concern himself with the Lord's affairs, and how he may please Him. But the married man is sure to be concerned also with matters of this world, that he may please his wife—his interests are divided. You find the same difference in the case of the*

unmarried and the married woman. The unmarried con-
cerns herself with the Lord's affairs, and her aim in life is
to make herself holy, in body and in spirit. But the mar-
ried woman must concern herself with the things of this
world, and her aim will be to please her husband (1 Corinthians 7: 32-34).

To twenty-first-century ears, that doesn't sound appealing. We aren't apt to find the idea of lifelong, single-hearted
devotion to God as an aim worthy of dropping every other
interest. But Paul's first-century audience would have heard
it much differently. Paul wrote at a time when the Church was
in crisis, evidently due to massive persecution. From the way
he writes, Paul seems to anticipate a rapid end, as though he
can hear the horsemen of the apocalypse in the distance. He
understood that the Church was in the midst of a crucial time,
that its response to the situation was pivotal, and that dedi-
cation to the faith was essential. His audience would have
understood this, too. Talking about forgoing marriage for the
sake of dedicating yourself to your faith is completely different to the guy in the recliner waiting for the Super Bowl to
start than it is to the guy wondering when he will be arrested, whether he will be killed, and what would happen to his
children if he did get married and have a family. Paul conveys
a sense of urgency:

All our futures are so foreshortened, indeed, that those
who have wives should live, so to speak, as though they
had none! There is no time to indulge in sorrow, no time
for enjoying our joys; those who buy have no time to
enjoy their possessions, and indeed their every contact
with the world must be as light as possible, for the pres-
ent scheme of things is rapidly passing away. That is why

I should like you to be free from worldly anxieties
(1 Corinthians 7: 29-32).

Paul also makes it clear that marriage is by no means wrong ("But if you, a man, should marry, don't think that you have done anything sinful" [v. 28]), and he encourages those who are married to stay married, even if their spouses do not believe in Christ ("If a brother has a non-Christian wife who is willing to live with him he should not leave her. A wife in a similar position should not leave her husband" [vv. 12-13]). Singleness may have been ideal under the circumstances, but those who were married shouldn't try to change their status.

SCHOOL FOR THE SPIRITUALLY INEPT?

Singleness is never disparaged in the Bible, at least for the sake of spirituality and the opportunities it affords to serve God. Singleness is presented as though it may be more beneficial for the Kingdom than marriage, especially at certain key times when Christians are facing persecution. Paul also thought we may be happier if we stayed single. Marriage is never equated with having attained a sufficient level of spiritual growth, and singleness is never deprecated as the school of instruction for those who just don't get the Christian life. Both are presented as legitimate alternatives for the mature Christian. Hsu quotes John Stott:

> ...If marriage is good, singleness is also good. It's
> an example of the balance of Scripture that,
> although Genesis 2:18 indicates that it is good to
> marry, I Corinthians 7:1 (in answer to a question
> posed by the Corinthians) says that "it is good for
> a man not to marry." So both the married and the

single state are good; neither is in itself better or worse than the other.[33]

Early Christianity encouraged and supported marriage and family, certainly, but in light of the family-dominated cultures around it, it presented singleness as a viable, good alternative, which might in fact make you more profitable in your Christian life—and happier—than marriage and family.

Marriage may be "normal." But singleness is good—sometimes better than marriage. It's a symbol of our wholeness and freedom in Christ.

Chapter Five

MARRIAGE ISN'T BETTER OR WORSE—IT'S DIFFERENT

❧

Marriage seems to be the promised land, the glorious happily-ever-after. The "dweam wifvin a dweam," to quote the priest from *The Princess Bride*. Marriage is someone to enjoy sex with, someone who will be glad to listen to office tales, someone to bring home a movie on Friday night. We tend to believe that marriage is better than singleness, that our married friends are better off than we are. Once we walk through those doors, the world will be transformed. We will be new, loved, whole. Marriage will fulfill that deep sense of longing and bring us peace. Even if we've been broken by an unsuccessful marriage, we may still hope in marriage's potential to heal us.

C.S. Lewis described his four-year marriage to Joy Davidman in *A Grief Observed*, the journal he wrote after she died: "The most precious gift that marriage gave me was this constant impact of something very close and intimate yet all the time unmistakably other, resistant—in a word, real."[34] We are each looking for someone different, someone outside of ourselves, with their own unique characteristics, yet so close as to be considered "one flesh." At times we are lost to the thought that we will never be complete or fulfilled if we don't find the right person.

How surprised would we be if we plunged into marriage and found life much the same—the old problems gone, perhaps, but new ones in their place? Found that you still have to brush your teeth in the morning, dishes still accumulate in the kitchen sink, and the process of two becoming one painfully wears down the rough edges you've become attached to?

We owe it to ourselves to try to understand what really happens in the happily-ever-after.

FOR BETTER

"I can't imagine not being married to Andrew. It's wonderful. We have so much fun together, and we enjoy the same things. For all that people talk about the problems of marriage and not wanting to lose their freedom, I wouldn't trade this for anything. It's not perfect, but it's so good."

Andrew and Katie don't go to marriage conferences or classes at church because the speakers and instructors tend to make marriage sound hard—and for them, it's not. Their theory is that if you think it's going to be hard, and you're looking for problems, you'll find them. They haven't found any yet, so they're not going to start looking.

Karen and Ben, married for 16 years, are still known to get starry-eyed in public, to want to share the backseat on a road trip so they can sneak in a kiss or two. They remark, "I have the best husband in the whole world," or "I have the best wife in the whole world." They both credit the strength of their marriage to their spouse. (Bring a strong stomach if you hang out with couples who display their feelings so publicly.)

Erica, a friend in her early 30's, gushed, "Everyone in the Christian world is so negative about the first year of marriage—they make it sound like it's so hard. We're having the time of our lives!"

No doubt, there are marriages in which "for better or for worse" tilts endurably to the nicer side of that equation.

C.S. Lewis described his marriage in more detail:

What was H. not to me? She was my daughter and my mother, my pupil and my teacher, my subject and my sovereign; and always, holding all these in solution, my trusty comrade, friend, shipmate, fellow-soldier. My mistress; but at the same time all that any man friend (and I have good ones) has ever been to me. Perhaps more. If we had never fallen in love we should have none the less been always together, and created a scandal.[35]

What more could anyone ask for?

God looked at Adam in the garden and declared that it was not good for him to be alone. God walking with him, or the animals around him, was not enough. He needed something more. So God created Eve, and thus, "For this reason a man will leave his father and mother and be united to his wife, and they will become one flesh" (Gen. 2:24).

Marriages like Lewis's, or Andrew and Katie's, or Ben and Karen's, make God's call to marriage seem just.

Yet, happily-ever-after is too simplistic to describe them. I hardly speak from authority, but it seems that even the best marriage will be fairly well beaten up at some time by the imperfections of the husband and wife. When large crises are scarce, the day-to-day effects of our humanness—our need for security, our selfishness, or even the fact that the clothes are dirty every week and the laundry must be done—can still be wearing.

Karen gets frustrated with Ben's need to analyze and rationally work through every conflict. "Ugh. I just want him to kind of bring it up, let me think about it, and then we can come back together and maybe talk about it some more, or maybe we won't even need to—maybe he'll be able to tell that I've been trying to do better. But it's not like that. I get the whole lecture. It's just the way he is."

Katie, an engineer, is a logical, organized planner. Andrew is less structured and takes his time—not necessarily aware of how much time he's taking, or what else needs to be done. When Andrew drives, he winds his way around until he figures out where he's going. Katie watches the map and figures out which turn Andrew *should* have taken at the last light. When we're all out backpacking, Andrew wants to go off the trail to explore the view from the rocks that hang over the cliff above the river. Katie has the guidebook out and knows we still have five miles to cover in the three hours of daylight left.

In *Good Will Hunting*, Robin Williams plays Sean, a psychiatrist whose wife died two years ago after a lengthy battle with cancer. Sean still misses her deeply; he doesn't want to marry again. They were so close, so much in love. In one of the best scenes in the movie, Sean is counseling Will, who hesitates to ask Skylar out again for fear of discovering that she's imperfect. Sean challenges Will with the idea that imperfections are "the good stuff" that love is all about:

> My wife used to fart when she was nervous. She had all sorts of wonderful idiosyncrasies. Know what? She used to fart in her sleep. ...One night it was so loud it woke the dog up. She woke up and go [sic] like, "Was that you?" I said, "Yeah," I didn't have the heart to tell her. ...She's been dead two years and that's the [stuff] I remember. Wonderful stuff, you know? Little things like that, those are the things I miss the most. The little idiosyncrasies that only I knew about, that's what made her my wife. Boy and she had the goods on me, too; she knew all my little peccadillos. People call these things imperfections. But they're not. Oh, that's the good stuff. And then we get to choose who we let into our weird little worlds.[36]

In a good marriage, two "weird little worlds" blend to become something better.

FOR WORSE

In *The Brothers K*, a modern American retelling of Dostoyevsky's classic, Marion Becker Chance, affectionately known as Grandawma, tries to set her young twin granddaughters straight on the fairy-tale story: "You think you'll grow up to marry a handsome prince, don't you? Well, let me tell you something, young lady. You shall, you shall. And *that's* when you'll find out that the fairy tale has it backwards. A few kisses, a few years—that's all it takes to turn the handsomest prince on earth into a big, ugly frog."[37] All joking aside, marriage can be the furthest thing from a fairy tale.

There are few great marriages in the Bible. Abraham and Isaac both tried to pawn their wives off as their sisters to spare their own lives. Jacob's wives—Leah and Rachel—were sisters and competitors of the worst kind. They married the same man within one week of each other. Rachel—the one Jacob loved—couldn't have children. Leah had four boys one after the other. Then they each gave Jacob their slaves to have children in their name. Can you imagine being one of those slaves, a pawn in a power struggle between two sisters, sleeping with a man who will never love you and never be your husband? Esther became queen, but she was taken into the king's courts by royal edict, not by choice, and shared her husband with as many women as he wanted. David won Michal, Saul's daughter, with the foreskins of 200 Philistines, and while they loved each other, they grew apart after David fled for his life.

We know the statistics—how many marriages end in divorce, even in the Church. We hear stories of marriages gone awry, wrecked by infidelity or just laziness. We're aware that a bad marriage would be worse than a lifetime of singleness.

Susan married at 40. David—prince charming in her estimation—went to church, he was respectful of Susan, he was fun. Susan expected life to be very good.

Marriage Isn't Better or Worse—It's Different

Two years later, there are days she would rather be dead than married. Her friends have urged her to move out, but she wants to fulfill her "for better or for worse" vow. She shared her story with me:

> I know you struggle with loneliness being single. Imagine being married, lying in bed at night next to someone, and feeling like there's an eight-inch space between you that's actually the size of the Grand Canyon. There's this lack of connection, and I can't get across it. I can't make him open up to me. It's the worst feeling in the world.
>
> We hear the marriage vows, and we think that it's for better, for richer, and for healthy. Let me tell you, it's not like that. There's another side to that story.
>
> We went through what I thought was extensive premarital counseling. Looking back, I can see that it wasn't as extensive as it should have been—it included nothing about one or both partners being divorced or having children, nothing about what it would mean to me to be a stepmother. We thought we were prepared, and I thought I knew who David was, what he valued. We were pursuing God together. It was fairly superficial, but trust and intimacy grow and deepen with time. I knew he had been deeply wounded in his first marriage, and I figured as long as we were headed in the right direction that love and time would take care of the rest and I had plenty of both...and a pretty unrealistic view of marriage....

My friends all had perfect marriages, and I
thought I would, too.

The Christian marriage books tell you that if you
do x, y, and z, your husband will respond appropriately, and it will all work out...It's not like that!
I can attempt to do x, y, and z, but he doesn't play
his part! And then I'm supposed to just continue
doing everything that's on my list of things to do
even though he doesn't do his. It's very difficult.
It's not the way they lead you to believe—it's just
not that easy....

If I didn't work, we wouldn't have a house. Christianity kind of teaches that if you're a woman, and
you're married, you should be the one homemak-
ing. And that's okay with me—I'm comfortable
doing that kind of thing, but he won't help. So
now I'm in a situation where I have to succeed in
both worlds. I have to bring home a paycheck, and
then I have to cook and clean and take care of
everybody. And it's not that he can't do that kind
of stuff, because he was on his own before he married me and he didn't starve and he had clean
clothes to wear, but now he just expects me to do it.

After they married, David became passive. He was laid
off from his job and took a year and a half to find a new one.
He's not interested in sex. He would rather take vacations
alone, and he lied to Susan about being on a business trip
when he was in Vail with a group of single friends. His daily
interactions with her show that she is not important to him.
She wonders now if he got married just so there would be

someone else to bring home a paycheck, fix dinner, and watch the kids. Susan feels emotionally abandoned.

Daniel e-mailed me distraught about the state of his marriage:

> My wife and I do not sleep together anymore, or
> rarely. It has been nearly two years since we had
> sex. To be honest with you, I am simply not
> attracted to her....she is overweight and doesn't do
> anything. She is often depressed and has fixed me
> probably ten to fifteen meals in the two years of
> our marriage. I cook for myself and her. She is on
> disability, partly for physical reasons, but she
> spends most of her time in bed during the day, not
> from necessity but from loss of interest in life....
> Lately, over the past month, there were about three
> or four times when I finally hit rock bottom emo-
> tionally, spiritually, and mentally. I had probably
> never been lower before in my entire life. I felt as
> though I had almost lost my faith as well. Nothing,
> absolutely nothing mattered to me. It was horrible
> and frightening.

In the movie *Enchanted April*, Lottie Wilkins experiences the same desperation: "...it's so cold having nothing on, and knowing that you'll never have anything on again. And you're going to get colder and colder, until at last you die of it. That's what it's like living with someone who doesn't love you."[38]

Obviously, these are extreme cases. And both Daniel and Susan would tell you they missed or ignored warning signs when they were dating. Their stories may prevent you from rushing down the aisle to someone you'd be better off to have as an acquaintance than as a soulmate.

IT'S NOT BETTER OR WORSE

"Marriage isn't better or worse; it's just different." I met Jen for coffee to talk about marriage. We've been through a lot together in the time we've been friends. We've shared the adventures of Internet start-up life and watched each other through a few relationships and the ongoing struggle of being content with singleness. Jen got married over a year ago. This is what she told me:

Marriage isn't better or worse; it's just different.
There are wonderful things about being married,
and wonderful things about being single—they're
just different gifts, and you have to recognize that,
and be thankful for the gifts you have now,
because they may not last forever....

I have to share every part of me with my husband.
It's not just a matter of sharing all your stuff, either;
it's sharing every deepest thought and motive.
When you live so closely with someone, you can't
conceal stuff. He sees the real you. All the good and
all the bad. It's an incredibly vulnerable place to be,
and I never expected that. It's terrifying. What if he
rejects you? What if he decides to leave? (Not that
that would happen, since you've both decided this
is a genuine commitment, but you can't help but
worry about that sometimes.)

I would tell you to seize the day—recognize the gifts God has given you now. It's a different gift, but it's still a gift. Focus on the blessings you have. You have to be secure in Christ. Even when you get married, that stays the same. Your marriage partner can't be your self-confidence, happiness, joy, security. Christ has to be that. Know that God wants what's best for you....

You feel an increased responsibility, or an increased awareness, that your relationship with Christ affects other people. It's a refining process. You know that saying, "Love is never having to say you're sorry"? Well, marriage is saying you're sorry over and over and over again. I see my selfishness, my black heart, my pride. It's humbling. Being married certainly has nothing to do with having spiritual superiority over single people. Anyone who thinks that is not being honest with themselves....

I think the worst moment in time for me was when I was in the bathroom of the townhouse we're living in now. I thought I had come to a place of contentment when I was single, but I realized then that there was a part of me that still thought marriage would bring the day-to-day happiness that, unbeknownst to me, I was still seeking. I realized then that marriage can't make you happy.

Perhaps most marriages fall into this category—they hit the extremes, the highs and lows, but spend most of their time with blessings and struggles in equal measure. Perhaps there's nothing inherently better about being married. William Backus, in his book *Telling Yourself the Truth*, confirms Jen's theory:

> Not long ago, a poll was taken of 5,000 middle-class single and married men and women....The poll revealed that single people were no more or less happy than the married people and the married people no more or less happy than the single. Common, however, was the finding that single people envied married people. Married people, on the other hand, reported envying single people. Many married people revealed that they were happy because they were "supposed to be happy," not because they actually had feelings of happiness in their lives.[39]

Someday, we may trade our singleness in for good things of the married sort, for debates over finances, and the pain and pleasure that come from living so closely with someone. Until then, we're not in such bad shape.

The Giant Crap Shoot

What are your chances of getting a marriage that's better, worse, or average? Brian used to say that the whole thing was a crap shoot: "No matter how well you think you know this person before you marry them, you really have no idea what you're getting. No idea. And even if you *do* know, they could change overnight. But I guess you have to roll the dice at some point. That's all it is—a giant crap shoot."

Marriage Isn't Better or Worse—It's Different

I'm sure there are Jekyll-and-Hyde stories about drastic changes on the other side of "I do," but there's a lot you can do to make sure you know what you're getting into.

Susan regrets not listening to the advice of her friends, who saw things in David that made them suspicious. They were alarmed by the fact that he didn't have any close friends, and they thought he seemed immature. Susan thought she knew better.

Her advice, as she explained it to me:

Ask your married friends if they have arguments. Find out how they resolved the last one. Ask them about the day-to-day reality of marriage. Do they have expectations of their marriage or spouse that aren't fulfilled?

My married friends always put their best side forward around me, and I thought they all had perfect relationships. I never saw any of their struggles. And it's really no fault of theirs—I'm sure they behave the same way no matter who they're around. None of us want to air our dirty laundry for everyone. But it left me with the impression that...the whole thing was wonderful. I just wish one of them had told me about the realities of it all. I wish I had known to ask.

When you meet someone who could be the right one for you, don't just do things alone as a couple. Get together with your friends so that they can get to know him. Listen to their advice. A lot of times your friends see things that you just can't see. Do things with his friends so you can get to know them, and get to know more about him through them. Pray. Listen to your parents, or if they aren't available, find an older mentor in your church who can advise you. Ask your pastor for his advice.

Daniel allowed himself to be pressured into his marriage: "I...married...under pressure from a local pastor because my girlfriend and I had been dating for a year and he said people might begin to 'talk' if we didn't get married. He thought the ideal state for Christians is marriage." When Daniel decided to call the wedding off, he met with resistance: "I went over to her apartment the next day to tell her. She was making plans for the wedding, but she could tell by looking at me that something was wrong. At first I just said that I wanted to put off the marriage. She threw a fit, almost had a psychotic episode...I didn't have the heart to break it off after that...."

If you decide the person you're dating or engaged to isn't right for you, there's nothing noble about marrying that person anyway.

Dennis Rainey, in *Preparing for Marriage*, stresses the value of preparation:

No other human relationship can approach the potential for intimacy and oneness that can be found within the context of the marriage commitment. And yet no other relationship can bring with it as many adjustments, difficulties, and even hurts. There's no way you can avoid these difficulties; each couple's journey is unique. But there is much you can do to prepare for that journey.[40]

Rainey's book arms couples with a set of exercises and questions—outlining your personal history, charting your life map, divulging your expectations, exploring communication styles, and discussing financial priorities—designed to help you decide if your relationship merits a hearty "I do!" and to prepare you for what you'll find on the other side of the marriage commitment. There are other similar books, and most churches offer premarital counseling that should achieve the same objective.

THE PURPOSE OF MARRIAGE

Stephen didn't get married until he was 40. He says that one of the things that kept him from getting married was his search for the perfect person. He could have been dating someone who met 95 percent of his expectations, but what if he married her and then met a 99 percent match? He'd be lost. He thinks most guys struggle with this; they may be happy in the relationship they're in, but there's a lurking fear that there may be someone better for them. That fear keeps them from committing.

Is marriage really about finding the perfect person?

Most often in the biblical stories, parents arranged for their children's marriages, not because that was a biblical mandate but because it was the custom. Abraham, who was too old to go himself, sent a servant back to his hometown to choose a wife for Isaac. Rebekah was chosen, and she left her family with one day's notice to move to a strange country and marry a man she'd never met. It seems that marriage, more than a romantic ideal, was a necessity of life.

Paul, though he praises singleness, encourages people to marry to avoid sexual sin. He encourages young widows to marry again to keep them from becoming lazy busybodies and gossips. He exhorts husbands to love their wives, and wives to respect their husbands. The marriage relationship is to be a picture of the relationship between Christ and the Church—Christ who came to serve, not to be served, even to give His life.

Though there are verses in Proverbs that warn us about the effects of a poor marriage choice (Proverbs 21:9: "Better to live on a corner of the roof than share a house with a quarrelsome wife"), there's no command or even guidance about finding the right person.

Many married friends I talk to share Jen's belief that God gives us marriage in order to help us become the person we need to be—that the daily interaction with someone so close, the constant feedback about what needs to change, and the awareness and exposure of thoughts and motives all serve to help us become more like Christ. Sheila Walsh shared her thoughts in a recent interview with Crosswalk.com: "I'm thankful for a husband who loves me on my good days and bad days. I'm thankful for an understanding that marriage isn't about making us happy, but about teaching us to be like Christ. It's not about making all my dreams come true. There's no greater forum to become like Christ, because there is no place where all my weaknesses are more exposed than in marriage."[41]

If the purpose of marriage is to become like Christ, then finding the perfect partner loses some of its importance— not that we should marry someone we do not love, but the difference between 95 percent compatibility and 99 percent compatibility becomes rather insignificant.

Henri Nouwen suggests that the purpose of marriage is for two people to create a place for God in the world:

> Marriage is not a lifelong attraction of two individuals to each other, but a call for two people to witness together to God's love. The basis of marriage is not mutual affection, or feelings, or emotions and passions that we associate with love, but a vocation, a being elected to build together a house for God in this world, to be like the two cherubs whose outstretched wings sheltered the Ark of the Covenant and created a space where Yahweh could be present (Exodus 25:10-12, I Kings 8:6-7).[42]

Marriage is not about me finding my fulfillment. It's about me playing the right part—the script God has written for me. It's about learning to love the way Christ loves, learning to serve, becoming humble, putting someone else first. Surely God will lead me to the right person if it is in His plan—someone I will love and care for deeply, who will help God whittle away at my heart, and who—no doubt—will turn out to be as far from perfect as I am.

PIECING TOGETHER THE TRUTH

Those of us who have never been married don't really know what marriage is like. It's a risky business trying to figure it out, given the fact that we probably can't understand it until we've lived through it. Asking friends helps us piece together the truth, though it's difficult because they all give us different answers, as every marriage is different. It may be wonderful. It may be horrible. It may be just okay. And it may be all three of those combined over a lifetime, or even in the same get-the-kids-to-school, dozen-roses, how-could-you-say-that week.

In the end, our marriages, like so many other areas of our lives, will be largely what we make them, and their substance will be determined by what we bring to them.

Susan challenges us to remember that we can't depend on marriage for salvation from a lesser life:

> If you're not a happy person as a single, marriage is not going to change that. If you have low self-esteem (or don't see yourself as God sees you), marriage is not going to change that. If you do not have intimate friendships as a single, marriage is not going to change that. If your walk with God is weak as a single, marriage is not going to change that. We need to pursue God—period. We need to become the person that God is molding us to be.

Chapter Six

You Are Fiercely Loved

⌘

I met Nancy at a retreat. Shortly into her marriage, her husband deserted her and their three children, two of whom had special needs. For 20 years, she took them to school, to church, to doctors and therapists, worked for their house and food, and watched them make good and bad choices out of her control—to have the baby, to finish school, to marry him anyway. Now that they're out of the house, Nancy wants to remarry. And now, at 50, there's no one around. Her voice hints at desperation: "I said to God, 'Okay, I did my time. I did my duty. Now it's my turn.' And there's no one there for me. I'm afraid I'm going to die never really knowing love." Nancy has expressed perhaps our greatest fear—to die without love.

It seems funny to talk about "dying without love" when you are loved immeasurably by God, the divine Creator, the One who fashioned your soul and drew up the template for your life.

God's love is deep enough to sit down in it, splash it around your arms and legs, relax, and breathe it in. You could float on your back and blow whale spouts with it. Some days we dive in, feel Him around us, and believe in His love. But often we tiptoe around the edges, wondering if we've really been given permission to swim.

According to the textbook, God's love is the truest we will ever know. Regardless of whether or not we marry, our relationship with Him will be the most meaningful of our lives. And yet, it is perhaps the hardest to get our hands around. I'm not sure why that should be. So much love, and we feel empty. Not all the time, but enough to wonder if we aren't missing something.

There are days when God's love is amazingly clear. Not long after Brian and I broke up, I wrote in my journal:

I am loved by God with an amazing, unbounded, all-knowing love. The beauty of that love brings me to tears even at the same time I'm mourning my own loss and my loneliness and pain. The depth of the pain and the depth of His love seem to meet in the same place in my heart, and it's more than I can handle.

Yet there are days I can't feel His love at all. A few years ago, I wrote:

Today God is to me an ogre, a demon. He is harsh, judgmental, cruel. He is frustrated with me because I never will live up to His standards. I set out to be like Him— even to be fully yielded to Him—and each day I come crawling back, a miserable failure. I am certain that He cannot be pleased to see me...

THE TRUEST LOVE

"Your love, O Lord, reaches to the heavens, Your faithfulness to the skies" (Ps. 36:5). The psalms are replete with this imagery. The love of God is bigger than the ocean. It's higher than the distance from me to the stars. It's wider than East to West.

And, John tells us that God *is* love (see 1 Jn. 4:8). Using Paul's explanation of love in First Corinthians 13, we know what God is like:

> God is slow to lose patience—He looks for a way of being constructive. He is not possessive...

> God has good manners and does not pursue selfish advantage. He is not touchy. He does not keep account of evil or gloat over the wickedness of other people. On the contrary, He shares the joy of those who live by the truth.

> God knows no limit to His endurance, no end to His trust, no fading of His hope; He can outlast anything. God never fails. (Based on 1 Corinthians 13:4-8a.)

I rewrite this so that it applies to me:

> God is slow to lose patience with me. He does not keep account of my evil or gloat over my wickedness. God shares my joy when I live by the truth.

It seems that the God who is, is different than the one in my head. I imagine Him to keep tabs on me, to tally my mistakes, to be exasperated with my continual failings, to even expect them. I sneak into my prayers in the morning, fearing that God remembers that I didn't have time for them yesterday, that my own lack of appreciation will have barred the door to grace. But what is He, really? He's patience. A clean slate. A cheerleader, even. If your spiritual life were the Marine Corps marathon, you get the feeling He'd be the sweaty-faced, camera-laden friend who hung around to see you finish just ahead of the rescue wagon.

The Wideness in God's Mercy

One of my friends introduced me to an old hymn about God's love when he rewrote the music and gave the words new life. It's become one of my favorites:

There's a wideness in God's mercy
like the wideness of the sea;
there's a kindness in His justice,
which is more than liberty.

There is no place where earth's sorrows
are more felt than up in heaven;
there is no place where earth's failings
have such kindly judgment given.

For the love of God is broader
than the measure of man's mind;
and the heart of the Eternal
is most wonderfully kind.

If our love were but more simple,
we should take Him at His word;
and our lives would be all sunshine
in the sweetness of our Lord.[43]

The unending mercy of God means that we will be accepted anytime we come back to Him—regardless of where we've been, or how often. We don't have to earn our salvation or God's love. David knew this forgiveness. He had called Bathsheba to his palace when her husband was out fighting in Israel's army. He slept with her; she got pregnant. David made sure her husband was killed in battle. Psalm 32 recounts his return to God's mercy:

> *Blessed is he whose transgressions are forgiven, whose sins are covered. Blessed is the man whose sin the Lord does not count against him and in whose spirit is no deceit. When I kept silent, my bones wasted away through my groaning all day long. For day and night Your hand was heavy upon me; my strength was sapped as in the heat of summer. Then I acknowledged my sin to You and did not cover up my iniquity. I said, "I will confess my transgressions to the Lord"—and You forgave the guilt of my sin....You are my hiding place; You will protect me from trouble and surround me with songs of deliverance (Psalm 32:1-5,7).*

In one movement of repentance, David went from carrying the weight of adultery and murder to deep intimacy with God.

Madeleine L'Engle, in her novel *A Live Coal in the Sea*, quotes William Langland's picture of the mercy of God: "But all the wickedness in the world which man may do or think is no more to the mercy of God than a live coal dropped in the sea."[44] When we resist the love of God, it is as though we are walking up to the waves on the beach with our small burning cinders, wondering if the ocean will be enough to put them out.

This overwhelming mercy drove Jesus to hang out with people whom the religious leaders of His day despised—prostitues, tax collectors, people plagued by demons. To others, they were unclean. To Him, they were vessels for mercy. Today, still, Jesus longs to acquaint Himself with people whom the offical Church voices may be tempted to judge harshly. Anne Lamott describes a key moment in her conversion story in her book, *Traveling Mercies*:

> I didn't go to the flea market the week of my abortion. I stayed home, and smoked dope and got drunk, and tried to write a little, and went for slow walks along the salt marsh with Pammy. On the seventh night, though, very drunk and just about to take a sleeping pill, I discovered that I was bleeding heavily. It did not stop over the next hour. I was going through a pad every fifteen minutes, and I thought I should call a doctor or Pammy, but I was so disgusted that I had gotten so drunk one week after an abortion that I just couldn't wake someone up and ask for help. I kept on changing Kotex, and I got very sober very quickly. Several hours later, the blood stopped flowing, and I got in bed, shaky and sad and too wild to have another drink or take a sleeping pill. I had a cigarette and turned off the light. After a while, as I lay there, I became aware of someone with me, hunkered down in the corner, and I just assumed it was my father, whose presence I had felt over the years when I was frightened and alone. The feeling was so strong that I actually turned on the light for a moment to make sure no one was there—of

course, there wasn't. But, after a while, in the dark again, I knew beyond any doubt that it was Jesus. I felt him as surely as I feel my dog lying nearby as I write this.

And I was appalled. I thought about my life and my brilliant hilarious progressive friends, I thought about what everyone would think of me if I became a Christian, and it seemed an utterly impossible thing that simply could not be allowed to happen. I turned to the wall and said out loud, "I would rather die."[45]

Abortion, drugs, alcohol—and Jesus. Jesus, who kept pursuing Anne even though she rejected Him that night in her loft. Jesus, who loves each of us, whether or not we love Him back appropriately. Such is the wideness of God's mercy.

God-Become-Flesh

Of course, Christ is the ultimate example of God's love. That the Creator should live among His creation, become one of them, and then allow them to kill Him unmercifully, to take the punishment we all should have received, to live the perfect life in order to die on our behalf, to kill death so that we would never know its power—this is amazing, deep, wade-through-it kind of love.

Isaiah 53 poetically tallies the Christmas score: He was despised; we esteemed Him not. He took our infirmities, carried our sorrows. He was pierced for our transgressions. He was bruised for our iniquities. His punishment brought us peace. His wounds brought us healing. We all went astray. He was crushed. We committed all the vile acts. His was all the suffering; ours, the salvation.

During the Christmas season, the celebration of God-become-flesh, I'm surrounded by the constant reminder of God's abounding mercy. I sit in the National Cathedral at midnight with my family on Christmas Eve, with the incense, the deep stained glass, the rising stone columns and the rose windows, and I know it's true, that God is love. I don't believe we could have dreamed up this kind of story about God—the Creator who limits Himself to our earthly, physical needs; allows us to kill Him unjustly; returns alive again, having conquered death, not to appear as a vengeful, judgmental spirit to those who nailed Him to the cross, but to a few of His followers, to encourage them to love Him, and to spread the word. He doesn't set up an earthly kingdom. He doesn't stop world history and call everyone to judgment. He slips away to Heaven, and says that someday He will be back, and, until then, the message is all mercy and grace.

Hosea & Gomer

Many of the words and stories that we use to talk about God's love are so overused and worn out that they lose their meaning. When you sit in church from age 3 on—or even from 15 on—words like *grace, mercy, love,* and *forgiveness,* the story of David's repentance, the words of Paul ("by grace you are saved"), the "Amazing Grace," you sing about, these things become part of your spiritual vocabulary. We talk about them with such regularity—and we should, because they're central to our faith—that perhaps we lose the ability to understand them. Even the story of Christ may lose its power. It seems grander at Christmas and at Easter, but it can seem unconnected to our daily lives.

It's important to find stories that give us fresh images of God's love. Anne Lamott's story does that for me, as does the picture of Christ, God-become-flesh, hanging out with sinners, going where mercy was most needed, being anti-religious-establishment because the establishment knew nothing of love, only works.

Another story that breaks through for me is the story of Hosea and Gomer. Hosea was a prophet during a time when Israel had become rich and self-satisfied, disregarding God. God compared His people to a faithless wife, one who didn't stop with loving other men but prostituted herself, losing all dignity and self-worth. To demonstrate His love for Israel, God called Hosea to marry a whore, to love her, and to have children with her. When she rejected everything Hosea had given her and went back to her old life, he was commanded to purchase her back and to set her in a place of honor. To everyone around him, Hosea was a fool. But it was the picture that God needed. Become the worst sort of people you can imagine. Run deliberately as far away from God as you can. He will not only love you still, but He will seek you out. And He longs for you to come back.

Everyday Grace

People come up to my mom and say, "You have such a wonderful daughter." And she's been known to smile and respond: "Ah, well, you don't really know her." It's a bit of a joke, but there's truth in it. I have a feeling that God would respond the same way. I come across as wholeheartedly committed, and yet there are all these things underneath that no one else sees. And that's what scares me. I'm fairly comfortable with the fact that I could walk away from the faith for a period of time and come back to God's open arms. What I have the most difficult time with is the daily things—the daily sins. God could forgive murder, but can He forgive my pride? Even when I do good things, part of me does them only because I want to be recognized for them. I believe that salvation is only through grace, and yet I try to earn His love. Paul talks about becoming a new creation when you accept God's grace—about how all the old things are gone, and the new are come. I don't really understand his meaning. It's as though God has picked up a corner of my soul to show me the muck underneath, to remind me that I'm not all I think I am. I worry about the things that I know are there—pride, anxiety, greed, the desire to follow God as long as I can do so comfortably, a willingness to forgive as long as the other person demonstrates sufficient anguish for what he or she has done—and then I worry about all the things under the covers that only God knows about. How can He forgive them?

There's a simple verse kids learn in Sunday school: "But if we freely admit that we have sinned, we find Him reliable and just—He forgives our sins and makes us thoroughly clean from all that is evil" (1 Jn. 1:9). We understand that in order to be forgiven, we must only ask. Traditionally, we're taught to confess our sins every evening. And yet, I think it may not be a nightly prayer, but something as constant as breathing, as regular as our sin. Perhaps we struggle to believe in a love that can handle that kind of need because we could never handle it ourselves. And God is so far beyond us that we will never understand the way He loves. Kierkegaard spoke of the leap of faith necessary to trust in God's grace for salvation. That big leap may be only the beginning; we are always taking tiny leaps of faith to believe that God will forgive us, that He will thoroughly clean us.

Paul encourages us in Romans to hold this incomprehensible love securely, without fear, to "hold our heads high":

> *Since then it is by faith that we are justified, let us grasp the fact that we have peace with God through our Lord Jesus Christ. Through Him we have confidently entered into this new relationship of grace, and here we take our stand...Yet the proof of God's amazing love is this: that it was while we were sinners that Christ died for us. Moreover, if He did that for us while we were sinners, now that we are men justified by the shedding of His blood, what reason have we to fear the wrath of God? If, while we were His enemies, Christ reconciled us to God by dying for us, surely now that we are reconciled we may be perfectly certain of our salvation through His living in us.* **Nor, I am sure, is this a matter of bare salvation— we may hold our heads high in the light of God's love because of the reconciliation which Christ has made** (Romans 5:1-2,8-11).

Now that we have accepted God's grace, what reason do we have to fear the wrath of God? None, Paul implies. We are secure. Not just eternally, but daily.

THE FIERCEST LOVE

An honest discussion of the love of God would not be complete without acknowledging the fact that God does not always act in ways that seem, well, loving. This God-become-flesh, abounding in grace, who bore all of our sorrows, doesn't seem to be able to stop the daily pain of life. Or chooses not to. There are parents who die of heart attacks or brain tumors. Friends who nudge their way into your heart, only to walk away suddenly, abruptly, violently, leaving your tenderest parts exposed. And numerous half-full queen-sized beds whose occupants hope to meet someone before they are 30...40...50.

The Problem of Pain

So, this God of love allows dreams that will never be met and relationships that cause immeasurable pain. The conflict this creates is traditionally referred to as the problem of pain: Because God allows terrible things to happen, He cannot be both all-powerful and loving. He must be one or the other.

C.S. Lewis addresses this issue extensively in his book, *The Problem of Pain*. Because Lewis believes that God is both all-powerful and loving, he suggests that our definition of love needs to be revisited. Here we begin to get the sense that we have gotten more than we bargained for:

> And by Love, in this context, most of us mean
> kindness—the desire to see others than the self
> happy; not happy in this way or that, but just
> happy. What would really satisfy us would be a
> God who said of anything we happened to like
> doing, "What does it matter so long as they are
> contented?" We want, in fact, not so much a Father
> in Heaven as a grandfather in heaven—a senile
> benevolence who, as they say, "liked to see young

people enjoying themselves," and whose plan for
the universe was simply that it might be truly said
at the end of each day, "a good time was had by
all." Not many people, I admit, would formulate a
theology in precisely those terms: but a conception
not very different lurks at the back of many minds.
I do not claim to be an exception: I should very
much like to live in a universe which was gov-
erned on such lines. But since it is abundantly
clear that I don't, and since I have reason to
believe, nevertheless, that God is Love, I conclude
that my conception of love needs correction.[46]

Lewis continues to argue that because God loves us, and
we are in essence His artistic masterpiece, He will not be content with us until we are what He wants us to be. The pain we
experience may be the tools in His arsenal—the potter's
mucky, molding hands; the kiln; the jeweler's fire to remove
the dross:

We are, not metaphorically but in very truth, a
Divine work of art, something that God is making,
and therefore something with which He will not be
satisfied until it has a certain character....

We are bidden to "put on Christ," to become like
God. That is, whether we like it or not, God
intends to give us what we need, not what we now
think we want. Once more, we are embarrassed by
the intolerable compliment, by too much love, not
too little."[47]

99

It is as though the parent/child relationship has been carried to its furthest extreme. A parent allows the child to experience pain (an hour in the child's room, a choking first draught on a cigarette) because the pain will help guide that child in a good way. And God allows us to experience the same kind of pain, designed to rid us of our old selves and make us into what we need to be—but He has a far greater knowledge of our character, knows how much pain we can bear, and knows exactly what the results will be.

This Love—the truest we will ever know—is also the fiercest. It's not the Sunday-afternoon kind of love that wants to order Chinese food and read the paper. It doesn't overly concern itself with our physical or emotional comfort, though that makes it sound as if it doesn't consider those at all, and I believe it does. I'll never forget a solo trip to Paris a few years ago in which God seemed to arrange all the details—a room with a view of the Eiffel tower; a chance to hear Brahms and Vivaldi in the tiny, beautiful, stained-glass Sainte-Chappelle; last-minute train tickets to Giverny to catch Monet's garden in full bloom. Those things are what we would call loving, but they don't seem to be the best kind of love, because they aren't Love's highest priority in our lives. Its highest priority is the well-being of our soul.

The Problem of Judgment

It seems that we should be able to assure ourselves of God's love and move on, yet there is one other aspect of God's character that I feel I have to address because it has a tendency to get in the way of my believing in His love: His judgment and the way it seems to be arbitrarily applied. He is, after all, the God of Sodom and Gomorrah, the great flood, Ananias and Sapphira, and, of course, hell.

Ann Lamott recognized an arbitrariness in the God that her Catholic childhood friend believed in:

> Looking back on the God my friend believed in, he seems a little erratic, not entirely unlike her father—God as borderline personality. It was like believing in the guy who ran the dime store, someone with a kind face but who was always running behind and had already heard every one of your lame excuses a dozen times before—why you didn't have a receipt, why you hadn't noticed the product's flaw before you bought it. This God could be loving and reassuring one minute, sure that you had potential, and then fiercely disappointed the next, noticing every little mistake and just in general what a fraud you really were. He was a God whom his children could talk to, confide in, and trust, unless his mood shifted suddenly and he decided instead to blow up Sodom and Gomorrah.[48]

As Lewis said, "And here is the real problem: so much mercy, yet still there is Hell."[49]

This issue is bigger than I will be able to cover here, but I think it's worth mentioning because there are signs in the stories of God's judgment that show that what we view as an unfeeling fire from Heaven is far from that—it is grieved, delayed as long as possible, and tempered by mercy and grace.

In the story of Sodom and Gomorrah, we get two pictures of the same God: the God who destroys, and the God who comes for dinner. The Lord sits with Abraham outside his tent and tells Abraham that He will go to Sodom and Gomorrah to see if their sin is really so bad. What follows after that is a wonderful scene where Abraham asks the Lord whether or not He will destroy the righteous along with the wicked, and barters Him down from 50 righteous necessary to save the city to only 10. I find comfort in Abraham's words in verse 25:

> *"Far be it from You to do such a thing—to kill the righteous with the wicked, treating the righteous and the wicked alike. Far be it from You! Will not the Judge of all the earth do right?"* (Genesis 18:25)

Sodom and Gomorrah were destroyed, but only after God had made an appearance, to see if there were any hope— and after Abraham knew that this was a God he could talk to, debate with even. It's interesting to see the juxtaposition of these two images of God—the God who sends down fire from Heaven, and the God who allows Himself to be questioned. The two images don't fit together in our minds, and perhaps that's the reason they're both included in this story, to give us hope that though God judges—harshly, at times—He is still approachable.

The story of Jeremiah offers further clues to God's methods. God pleaded with Judah for more than 20 years through Jeremiah. Even at the end, when the destruction of Judah had begun, He sent Jeremiah out yet again to stand in the temple, to plead, still hoping that they would change their hearts:

> *...Stand in the courtyard of the Lord's house and speak to all the people of the towns of Judah who come to worship*

in the house of the Lord. Tell them everything I command you; do not omit a word. Perhaps they will listen and each will turn from his evil way. Then I will relent and not bring on them the disaster I was planning because of the evil they have done (Jeremiah 26:2-3).

Judah didn't change. Destruction came.

Working to spare the nations around Judah, God sent them word through Jeremiah:

Do not listen to your prophets, your diviners, your interpreters of dreams, your mediums or your sorcerers who tell you, "You will not serve the king of Babylon." They prophesy lies to you that will only serve to remove you far from your lands; I will banish you and you will perish. But if any nation will bow its neck under the yoke of the king of Babylon and serve him, I will let that nation remain in its own land to till it and to live there, declares the Lord (Jeremiah 27: 9-11).

Jeremiah gives us a picture of a God who pleads and provides a way of escape.

Jonah's story is the most encouraging. God used Jonah to show compassion on Israel's enemies. Like Sodom, Ninevah's wickedness got God's attention. He asked Jonah to visit Ninevah and tell them of its impending destruction. The story is well known: Jonah ran in the opposite direction, was swallowed by a great fish, then agreed to do as God had asked him. When the whole city of Ninevah repented, God spared their lives, and Jonah became angry:

> ..."O Lord, is this not what I said when I was still at
> home? That is why I was so quick to flee to Tarshish. I
> knew that You are a gracious and compassionate God,
> slow to anger and abounding in love, a God who relents
> from sending calamity" (Jonah 4:1-2).

Jonah understood God's character enough to know that
God is a God who relents, even with our enemies.

Although these stories give me hope, there are days
when I think about Ananias and Sapphira, about Moses' hit-
ting the rock and not being allowed into the promised land,
and wonder if I don't trespass on God's justice the same way
they did—and merit the same response.

Then I think about David sleeping with Bathsheba;
about Peter saying, "I never knew Him," just before he heard
the rooster crow for the third time; about Sarah laughing
when she heard she would have a child in her old age; about
Joseph's ten brothers—from whom came 10 of the 12 tribes—
selling Joseph into slavery and then telling their father he'd
been killed. And I think that I am in good company, company
that can only afford to hope in the God who is "compassionate and gracious, slow to anger, abounding in love," who
"does not treat us as our sins deserve or repay us according
to our iniquities" (Ps. 103:8,10).

BREATHING IT IN

God is "gracious and compassionate, slow to anger and
rich in love" (Ps. 145:8). Yet He is also "great in power" and
"will not leave the guilty unpunished" (Nahum 1:3). We can't
understand how these two aspects of God's character work

together, but we can stand confidently in His grace and "hold our heads high in the light of God's love," as Paul directed.

We may not always understand the methods of God's love: the way it pursues us, the way it pushes and pulls us and bends us, to make us into something different and better. We may want, at times, to get out from under its fierce gaze. But we may always be assured of its presence. To quote Lewis again:

> When Christianity says that God loves man, it means that God loves man: not that He has some "disinterested," because really indifferent, concern for our welfare, but that, in awful and surprising truth, we are the objects of His love. You asked for a loving God: you have one. The great spirit you so lightly invoked, the "lord of terrible aspect," is present: not a senile benevolence that drowsily wishes you to be happy in your own way, not the cold philanthropy of a conscientious magistrate, nor the care of a host who feels responsible for the comfort of his guests, but the consuming fire Himself, the Love that made the worlds, persistent as the artist's love for his work and despotic as a man's love for a dog, provident and venerable as a father's love for a child, jealous, inexorable, exacting as a love between the sexes. How should this be, I do not know: it passes reason to explain why any creatures, not to say creatures such as we, should have a value so prodigious in their Creator's eyes. It is certainly a burden of glory not only beyond our deserts but also, except in rare moments of grace, beyond our desiring...But the

fact seems unquestionable. The Impassible speaks as if it suffered passion, and that which contains in Itself the cause of its own and all other bliss talks as though it could be in want and yearning."[50]

Chapter Seven

You CAN Be Content

❧

It's impossible for me to talk about contentment without feeling like my mother. *Contentment* is a mother word—along with *homework*, *broccoli*, and *character-building experience*. To compound the problem, the verses about contentment imply that we should go about this wholeheartedly—we should joyfully welcome pain, always be rejoicing, always giving thanks.

It's the spiritual equivalent of working out—you know you should do it, but it's not inherently appealing. Like the Bally body everyone wants, no one really wants to do the work to get there (and although contentment may require as much work as perfectly toned abs, it doesn't get stares on the street). Bottom line: contentment means hard work, and the payoff seems questionable.

What You Really Want

Why should you care? Because contentment is what we're all looking for, whether we know it or not. We give it names—different names for each of us, and different sometimes from day to day or year to year. We deem it "a date Friday night" or "an afternoon in the sun on the pink Bermuda sand" or maybe "an arm around me at 6 a.m. in the quiet morning." Sometimes we get even more specific: the bookish one in accounting, the guy who leads worship, the flirtatious friend. We name it these things to make it tangible. We track its patterns in the lives of others and imagine how it will be for us: It will arrive on the Red Line at Union Station, we will bump into it in line at Starbucks on the way to work, and life will change. It is happiness, by definition. And until it comes, we sit and wait.

The thing we want, though, is the happiness itself, the contentment—not the *nom du jour* we've given it. Contentment is available without any of the extra packaging; it's elusive. Look for it in the Friday night date or the marriage proposal and it might not be there—and it might be too late for you to get out. Find it now, and it will be a constant companion. Expect it to come later, and it may always elude you.

WHAT IT IS

The Definition

Contentment is being okay with something (or a lot of things) you're not okay with. It's being satisfied with what you have. It's the ability to open up wide and swallow whole the lot life has given you.

Sound appealing? Maybe not. Still, give it a chance. Too many people I talk to sit out weddings or vacations or solo trips to the movies because they're discouraged. If you're in their situation, contentment may mean getting your life back.

One guy shared in the Crosswalk.com forums that he skipped his best friend's wedding because he couldn't stand the pain:

> On Memorial Day weekend, I "chickened out"—I
> did not show up for my best friend's bachelor
> party nor did I show up for his wedding. I WAS
> WRONG! Why? Because I could not bear the
> agony of going alone nor could I face my current
> state of singleness when two become one.

I've suffered through enough baby showers and bridesmaid dresses to know that when you aren't content with your singleness, it's impossible to share the joy of others.

Contentment is being able to laugh with a friend when her fiancé throws out all of the pew bows she stayed up until 3 a.m. making. It's being close enough to hear those stories, rather than avoiding the details and showing up at the wedding as though it were a pulling-off-a-Band-Aid experience. Contentment is a Friday-night sigh of relief to be home alone. It's being able to enjoy a niece's baby shower, a friend's new house, a brother's successful business. It's a security in who you are that enables you to experience the compounded joy of friends' triumphs. It's the ability to look peacefully at the future.

Contentment is beauty. People who are content radiate peace, a warm acceptance of life, and love and concern for others.

It's a Decision, Not a Feeling

Contentment is a determination of the will. It's not a higher state of consciousness in which you never again desire what you don't have. It's not waking up every day to sun-shine with a smile on your face.

Some days, it's realizing that you're about to turn 37 and the biological clock you thought had settled down is about to explode. It's having to go through all those feelings one more time. It's determining to deal with it one more time.

It doesn't always feel good.

The feelings often come, though, after the determination is made. In my own life, the more I've stretched and toned my contentment muscles, the more content I feel for longer peri-ods of time. But then I'm hit with a gut-pinching realization that I am alone, that all would be better if I could just have that fabric-softener-cologne-deodorant smell of a hug...and I get ready for another round.

To be content is to accept the gifts of God with thankful-ness and a willingness to do His will. You don't have to feel like it. You just have to do it.

WHAT IT S NOT

"I'm okay, I'm okay, I'm okay"

Some of the e-mail I get from readers concerns me. They seem to be stuffing down all of their pain, putting a good face on it, and calling it contentment.

You can't tell yourself you're okay without dealing with the pain you've been through or with the longings you strug-gle with every day. You have to face up to them. Otherwise, you don't have contentment. Instead you have a fantasy world in which you learn over and over again to ignore your deepest feelings and pretend they don't exist. It's a recipe for emotional disaster.

Ironically, at some point, contentment requires the ability to be broken and needy. If you can't admit your own brokenness, you can't accept it. You can't determine to be thankful for it.

It's Not Dependent on What You Have

It's tempting to think, "If only I were married, I'd be happy." But (so my friends tell me) the coveted item changes. The mantra becomes, "If only I had kids...." And then, "If only my kids would behave..." or "If only my husband would respect me...." We're always one step away from what will make us happy.

A number of married people e-mailed me to tell me contentment didn't meet them at the altar:

- Your article reminded me again that being "alone" isn't just connected with singleness or marriedness. I have felt as much or more "alone" while being married than I did while I was single. While single I had a great social/support network....

- I think it's important to realize that the issues of adequacy, contentment, and Christ-centeredness that you talk about are not at all unique to singleness. Any Christian struggles with these same issues—they are a part of spiritual growth and I would hesitate to call any faith genuine if it didn't spend a measure of time grappling with them.... even in marriage, the need for GOD is not met. A married person, as much as a single person, must daily recognize Christ as the source of help and contentment. I really don't want to minimize the special struggles of a single woman, but I do want to remind you that we're all in this together! The mystery of finding contentment and fulfillment in Christ is one we can all relate to.

✦ I enjoyed your column and I do believe everyone could enjoy contentment. I just haven't found it. The only time in my life I was ever contented was when my three children were born. Raising them gave me great pleasure. Now my oldest is in the Air Force. I have two still at home....They are at an age that they don't need me as much....My husband is off doing his own thing, as always. Frankly I don't know what it is that I want to do. I feel inadequate and have a very low self esteem about myself....

Everyone struggles with contentment. Don't slip into thinking that this conflict is unique to singles or that you'll be able to leave it behind with your single friends when you slip on a wedding ring.

It Doesn't Eliminate Your Desires or Your Past Hurts

Contentment isn't about getting rid of your desires or pretending that you don't want to get married. It doesn't remove the pain of divorce. Contentment and your desires and hurts can coexist. They should coexist. You can't eliminate your feelings, and you shouldn't try.

Sometimes we think that if we desire something we don't have, we can't be content. Jim fell for that lie, as he shared in an e-mail to me:

> I think that singles who are so super spiritual that they don't want a relationship with a member of the opposite sex are hiding behind their Lord to cover their own inadequacies. I would like to be married and I don't think that the super spiritual singles have a right to tell me that I should be content being single.

Jim has a point. Some people, trying to grasp contentment, push down all their longings and pretend they aren't there. Jim doesn't believe he can be content because he wants to be married. Both are wrong.

Lara struggled with this distinction, too:

> I get very frustrated when people try to make my desire for a husband sound like either a lack of trust in God or not allowing God to meet all my needs. I am satisfied—MORE than satisfied with all that God has provided me, but I will not feel guilty for my desire for a partner here on earth.

The example of Christ the night before He died is the best example of this delicate balance. He begged God to let this cup—His crucifixion—pass from Him. He spent the night before He was arrested praying desperately that God would take it away. He sweat blood. But He determined to be content with the fact that He had to face Golgotha, the vinegar, the spear, the dark cloud of His Father's abandonment. He would only be content with God's will:

"My heart is breaking with a death-like grief"..."My Father, if it is possible let this cup pass from Me—yet it must not be what I want, but what You want."..."My Father, if it is not possible for this cup to pass from Me without My drinking it, then Your will must be done" (Matthew 26:38-42).

Was Christ content going to the cross? Yes. But it wasn't easy for Him.

And though our burden pales in comparison, it won't be easy for us, either.

It's okay to struggle. It's okay to want to get married—it doesn't nullify your contentment. Don't let satan tell you otherwise.

WHAT IT REQUIRES

Complete Abandonment to the Will of God

An angel appeared in Mary's room and told her she would have a son who would be Jesus, the Lord, the Savior of His people. Mary wasn't sure what to make of this—in the first place she wasn't married and she wasn't sure why the angel would have called her "favored one" and said, "the Lord is with you!" The angel told her, "The Holy Spirit will come upon you, the power of the Most High will overshadow you. Your child will therefore be called holy—the Son of God....no promise of God can fail to be fulfilled" (Lk. 1:35-37).

Mary's response is beautiful: "I belong to the Lord, body and soul,...let it happen as you say" (Lk. 1:38). Her life had just gone from normal, predictable, and quiet to out of control and impossible to explain. She would be pregnant and unmarried. Joseph would have every right to send her away. She would carry the social stigma of being an unwed mother. She doesn't doubt that what the angel said would happen. She doesn't withhold herself from any part of it. Her heart is full of praise.

Mary's words carry the weight of a resolute decision she must have made long ago. She didn't have to think about her response. She knew that she was God's. She knew that she would do anything God wanted her to. If the angel had said, "Mary, tomorrow you'll die for your faith," her answer would have been the same: "I belong to the Lord, body and soul, let it happen as you say." Mary had abandoned herself to God's will for her life.

We need Mary's abandonment. We need to throw ourselves open to whatever God has for us, to be able to pray "let it happen as You say"—whatever that means for our lives.

A "Prayer of Abandonment" by Charles de Foucauld, a monk, echoes Mary's heart:

Father, I abandon myself into Your hands;
do with me what You will.

Whatever You may do,
I thank You.
I am ready for all,
I accept all.

Let only Your will be done in me,
and in all Your creatures.
I wish no more than this, O Lord.

Into Your hands
I commend my soul.
I offer it to You
with all the love of my heart.

For, I love You, Lord,
and so need to give myself,
to surrender myself into Your hands
without reserve
and with boundless confidence.

For You are my Father.[51]

When I am discontent, I pray this monk's prayer. It affirms the things I know but forget in the barrage of daily emotions: My life belongs to my Father and Lord. I love Him with all my heart. I want Him to do whatever He will with me. I pray, and peace floods my spirit.

Recognizing the Value of What You Have

"The Lord is my shepherd, I shall not be in want." David recognized that God would meet all of his needs. God restored his soul, went with him through the worst circumstances, taught him to live rightly, and gave him an abundance of goodness and love and the prospect of an eternity in His house. All of this, and David wanted nothing else. He says in Psalm 16:

Lord, You have assigned me my portion and my cup; You have made my lot secure. The boundary lines have fallen for me in pleasant places; surely I have a delightful inheritance (Psalm 16:5-6).

David goes on later to explain exactly why he feels so fortunate:

Therefore my heart is glad and my tongue rejoices; my body also will rest secure, because You will not abandon me to the grave, nor will You let Your Holy One see decay. You have made known to me the path of life; You will fill me with joy in Your presence, with eternal pleasures at Your right hand (Psalm 16:9-11).

David's deepest needs were filled by God, not by the things God gave him. He valued his relationship with God above everything else.

My own relationship with God is turbulent. My journal entries range from despondent ("Today God is to me an ogre, a demon. He is harsh, judgmental, cruel") to joyful ("I am loved by God with an amazing, unbounded, all-knowing love"). David loved God with all his heart, but he didn't always understand Him, and he often lost sight of Him. The same David who gave us Psalm 23's picture of rest ("The Lord is my shepherd, I shall not be in want") also gave us Psalm 22, which begins with the cry of desperation Jesus echoed on the cross:

My God, my God, why have You forsaken me? Why are You so far from saving me, so far from the words of my groaning? O my God, I cry out by day, but You do not answer, by night, and am not silent (Psalm 22:1-2).

Yet, David's soul and body longed for God (see Ps. 63:1), so he kept pursuing.

The Single Truth

In Psalm 73, Asaph talks about his struggles with jealousy after watching the success of the wicked and the unfairness that set off the writer of Ecclesiastes:

> *But as for me, my feet had almost slipped; I had nearly lost my foothold. For I envied the arrogant when I saw the prosperity of the wicked. They have no struggles; their bodies are healthy and strong. They are free from the burdens common to man; they are not plagued by human ills....This is what the wicked are like—always carefree, they increase in wealth. Surely in vain have I kept my heart pure; in vain have I washed my hands in innocence. All day long I have been plagued; I have been punished every morning* (Psalm 73:2-5, 12-14).

Karen echoed Asaph's frustration in her e-mail to me: "I really wrestle with contentment. I know that most of us do. But what I am so...I guess, angry about...is that I have done all the 'right things.' " Maybe you can relate: "God, I did everything right. My friends who went off and did their own thing are happy. They're not alone. What about me? I followed You...for nothing."

Asaph continues by looking at the final end of the wicked, and he concludes with God's sufficiency:

> *When I tried to understand all this, it was oppressive to me till I entered the sanctuary of God; then I understood their final destiny. Surely You place them on slippery ground; You cast them down to ruin....Yet I am always with You; You hold me by my right hand. You guide me with Your counsel, and afterward You will take me into glory. Whom have I in heaven but You? And earth has*

nothing I desire besides You. My flesh and my heart may fail, but God is the strength of my heart and my portion forever. Those who are far from You will perish; You destroy all who are unfaithful to You. But as for me, it is good to be near God. I have made the Sovereign Lord my refuge; I will tell of all Your deeds (Psalm 73:16-18, 23-28).

We have access to the same God. It is good to be near Him. He is our guide and constant companion. He watches over us carefully. He restores our souls, so we are fully known and fully forgiven. We will never be without His presence, His guidance, His love, or His best for our lives. They are all we need. With them, we lack nothing essential. We don't always understand Him, but our souls and bodies long for Him, so we keep pursuing.

Seeing Good in Bad

As you may have guessed, it doesn't stop there. The radical Christian perspective on life calls us to recognize eternal value in things that are downright painful.

Paul mastered this. He chose to be satisfied ("well-pleased" is the actual translation of the Greek word) with the thorn in his flesh, although he prayed that God would take it away:

Three times I begged the Lord for it to leave me, but His reply has been, "My grace is enough for you: for where there is weakness, My power is shown the more completely." Therefore, I have cheerfully made up my mind to be proud of my weaknesses, because they mean a deeper

experience of the power of Christ. I can even enjoy weak-
nesses, insults, privations, persecutions and difficulties
for Christ's sake. For my very weakness makes me strong
in Him (2 Corinthians 12:8-10).

Paul also learned to view his imprisonments as something good. He writes in the letter to the Philippians,

Now I want you to know, my brothers, that what has
happened to me has, in effect, turned out to the advan-
tage of the gospel. For, first of all, my imprisonment
means a personal witness for Christ before the palace
guards, not to mention others who come and go. Then, it
means that most of our brothers, taking fresh heart in the
Lord from the very fact that I am a prisoner for Christ's
sake, have shown far more courage in boldly proclaiming
the Word of God (Philippians 1:12-14).

One of my closest friends was diagnosed with a large,
most likely malignant tumor at 24. "I don't understand Christians. Everybody's praying that I'll get better. Why? Why
don't they pray about what I'm going through, that I'll be
able to learn what God has for me? God may heal me. But
He's doing so much more through this than just that."

The church's response was to pray for healing, but Anna
wanted more than that. She wanted to walk through the
depths of that experience. She knew it would change her life.
And she knew that she needed to be changed. She desperately longed to be more like Christ.

Today she would tell you, "Sometimes you pray for a
blessing and get a tumor—and it IS a blessing." She rejoiced
in what most of us would wish away.

To be truly content, we have to be able to see the value in our pain. God is at work. He doesn't waste our experiences. He's using them for a higher purpose that we can't always discern. We just have to have the faith to accept that and—eventually—to rejoice in that.

Taking Time to Learn

Toward the end of the Book of Philippians, Paul writes perhaps the best-known verses on contentment:

> ...I have learned to be content, whatever the circumstances may be. I know now how to live when things are difficult and I know how to live when things are prosperous. In general and in particular I have learned the secret of eating well or going hungry—of facing either plenty or poverty. I am ready for anything through the strength of the One who lives within me (Philippians 4:11-13).

Paul learned to be content in the varying circumstances he faced because of the power of Christ living in him. It's important to recognize that this takes time. Paul wrote these verses toward the end of his life. He'd been through shipwrecks, beatings, imprisonments, and near-death experiences. He learned contentment over a lifetime.

Someone told me, "You can do that now! You can be content right now because Christ is living in you! Like Paul said, 'I can do anything...'." I don't believe that. There are days I'm content, and there are days that contentment vanishes and I feel like I have to start all over. I think contentment is a spiritual discipline that requires a lot of time and exercise. I feel like I'm moving in the right direction, and, eventually, I may be able to echo Paul's words, but I won't be discouraged if it takes me a while to get there.

CONTENT WITH TODAY

Two weeks ago, the mulberry tree in my backyard was covered in fruit. The squirrels were incited to acrobatics by berries dripping off the branches. Berries littered the ground, the deck, and my neighbor's back porch. They were beautiful, lush, and inherently short-lived. Today the branches are bare.

I wonder if contentment isn't the mulberry of spiritual fruits. As soon as we produce it, it begins to rot and fall off the tree. We think we've arrived, but our branches are quickly stripped bare. We don't get to produce one permanent crop and move on. We can't afford to think that we have this one mastered.

The most difficult battle I face is the battle to be content with today, whatever today looks like every time I climb out of bed. To be content that I have to go to work, that I don't really enjoy my job right now, that I'd rather be doing something else, that a friend took an hour of my time to tell me everything about her life and didn't make me feel any better about mine, that I can't understand how a succession of individual days like this would ever add up to anything important. I may get together with an old friend, only to realize that her life is perfect and she has everything I ever wanted. I may just feel that sinking feeling deep inside and realize I've grown away from the contentment I thought I had.

Each day, I have to choose contentment. And for the big things in life, I'm going to have to choose it again and again and again.

IT'S POSSIBLE

My in-box is full of stories from people who have aspired to contentment. One such woman wrote to me:

> I struggled for twenty years with being single. I wanted God's will, but I wanted so desperately to get married. I could not understand why God would not give me a husband if He loved me. There were five basic things God taught me through my struggle that have been an encouragement to me....

She lists the sovereignty of God, her completeness in Him, the way He meets her needs, the way He loves her, and her need to encourage other struggling singles. She continues:

> I am truly content with being single. I never would have guessed that I could ever be happy being single, but I am realizing how much God loves me. My desire now is to love the Lord with all of my heart, soul, and might (Deut. 6:5) and work on developing a close relationship with Him. I am burdened for single women who think they have to get married to be happy. (And I get so frustrated when I hear someone say "if you want a husband, just pray and God will give you one." That is not necessarily true.) I try to encourage single women to trust God with this area of their life and allow Him to love them.

Others echo here theme:

+ I am recently divorced. I was married for sixteen years and have two kids. I eventually found out my ex-husband was living a double life and just figured out that he has probably done that since I've known him....I cannot explain how great my relationship is with God. I have learned over the years to completely turn to Him and rely completely on God for everything. It is amazing how content I feel in my life. I have peace and joy....I have told others how content I am and they have a hard time believing it. I do too compared to the way I used to feel without a guy in my life. I know the fulfillment comes from my relationship with God and all the blessings I have in my life and how everything has turned out.

- I am a pastor...that has been "single-again" for eleven years. I've really wrestled with the very issues you discuss. It has only been in the last three months that I have experienced the contentment that God has for me in my singleness. Once the contentment came into my life, there has been tremendous peace. I realize that I have a wonderful life and that even though I am not married, this is where God intends for me to be. WOW, what a release! God is good. Sometimes, knuckleheads like me are a little slow in realizing it though. If more Christian singles realized their completeness in God's plan they could be so much happier. Too many Christian singles try to live the expectations of other Christians and rush in another relationship or marriage just to feel complete. What a mistake!

No matter where you are right now, contentment is possible. And if you decide to try it, it will open your eyes to thousands of blessings that are hiding right under your nose.

WHAT DO YOU WANT YOUR LIFE TO BE LIKE?

As we sat over coffee, KC asked me bluntly: "So what do you want to be like if you don't get married? That's the question you have to face."

We were musing over the issue at hand: singleness and how to deal with it—the thing I kept giving to God and yet not really getting rid of in my heart.

"It's like a ball and chain," KC said. "You give it to God, you lay it at His feet, and when you get 20 or 30 feet away you realize that it's still got you."

Karen Clark, 38 and single, was well satisfied with her situation in life. She worked at the same harried pace that I did, and she'd been carrying this burden of singleness for much longer than I had, but she was completely at peace. She wasn't striving with the world. "What do you want to be like if you never get married?" She was the only friend bold enough to challenge me that way. I decided to try to be content, like Karen.

I hope you'll join me in the journey.

Chapter Eight

PURITY IS PART
OF YOUR SPIRITUAL CORE

❧

One night, after *Seinfeld*, I pushed away all the big pillows that were between Brian and me on the couch and put my head back on his shoulder. He put his arms around me—his fingers on my fingers, hands, arms—and for the first time our growing friendship had a physical outlet. I turned into a pile of mush, unable to move, unable to reason. A veteran of few serious relationships—and those mostly the Baptist "you can sit on the couch as long as there's a New Testament between you" variety—I was intoxicated, shocked, surprised by this force.

From that innocent exchange one Thursday night, we wandered into some more serious territory during the holidays and had several discussions about standards and limits, and eventually I decided that I could extend my comfort zone to encompass this realm of activity. I knew that Elisabeth Elliot recommended absolute purity before marriage, and I'd been faithful to that all my life. But I was 26, and I felt that I could handle it, and that I had some kind of right to it. By Valentine's Day, I was dragging myself from Brian's apartment, joking plaintively, "Okay, this is it...take me now or lose me forever!" But it wasn't always a laughing matter.

The whole relationship with Brian was one of setting standards and breaking them. Things went further than I ever intended them to. I recoiled from it at first, but it was enticing and warm and filling. I drew lines in the sand, determined to stop at a certain point, only to decide later that I shouldn't make it hard on myself. But I did make it hard on myself. I made promises to myself and to God, and I failed almost every time.

I found myself in the middle of this relationship that I thought was working the way it was all supposed to, yet somehow we couldn't manage this one thing. How could something that used to be clear-cut now be completely murky? How could I lack the willpower to choose my way in this one area?

Elisabeth Elliot, in *Passion and Purity*, describes our love lives, as Christians, as "a crucial battleground. There, if nowhere else, it will be determined as to who is Lord: the world, the self and the devil, or the Lord Christ."[52] I found that true, and I found myself completely unprepared for the conflict.

WHAT WE SAY AND WHAT WE DO

Perhaps it is obligatory that every Christian singles book address this topic and inevitable that it will come down firmly on the no-sex-before-marriage side. Although most Christians expect to hear this from the pulpit, it may not make sense to them in the midst of their lives, and many have decided that perhaps it's not so important after all.

Left alone with what we are made of—with the intoxicating, surprising touch, with the seething, under-the-surface sexuality that we try to ignore or avoid, with these 35-year-old virgin bodies—it may not seem so bad to take the easy way out, to give in. It seems that even God, who didn't equip us very well if He wanted us to wait until middle age for sex (or to abstain forever, perhaps, God forbid), would understand.

So, many single Christians—in college, young 20-somethings, established professionals—are concluding from their life experience and from some general if misinterpreted sense of the grace and kindness of God that sex is acceptable. They theorize: If you can't wait any longer, you shouldn't worry about it; God probably doesn't. And if there's any doubt in your mind about what God thinks about sex, why would you wait?

My friend Rachel attended a mega-church in the D.C. area, and brought her boyfriend, who had just become a Christian, to her Bible study. In addition to enhancing his overall spiritual growth, Rachel hoped for some affirmation of the sexual standards she'd grown up with, standards that seemed bizarre to her boyfriend. She was distraught to hear the Bible study leader tell the group that premarital sex wasn't an issue, that they shouldn't worry about it. Other recently engaged friends have been alarmed at the number of Christian couples who advise them to throw out the old standards now that they've got a formal commitment. One guy reader wrote me: "My position on the issue is that sex is OK provided there is a deep spiritual bond between the man and woman...."

Lauren Winner, in her Beliefnet essay "Sex and the Single Evangelical," describes the choices her friends have made:

> My unmarried evangelical friends, I think, are fairly representative. Some of them are virgins. Seriously chaste virgins. Others are virgins in Bill Clinton's sense: in the tactful euphemism of my friend Sheila, they "entertain through other orifices" nightly....

> Then there are those who do have sex, like Jill, a Wheaton college grad who lost her virginity in the Billy Graham Center.[53]

A recent Barna survey found that 36 percent of Christians—those "who said they have made a personal commitment to Jesus Christ that is still important in their life today"—believe that cohabitation before marriage is morally acceptable.[54]

Julia Duin discussed the statistics in her BreakPoint opinion piece, "No One Wants to Talk About It":

> I was not totally convinced that most women were out there doing it, so I started polling some of my born-again friends. Far fewer of them were virgins on their wedding nights than I had thought. One Catholic friend, who was trying to stay chaste, told me that even the priests in her life were suggesting she might try mutual masturbation with her boyfriend.

My research turned up a few rough figures. In their 1991 book, *Single Adult Passages: Uncharted Territories*, Carolyn Koons and Michael Anthony had surveyed 1,500 single Christians. They found significant levels of sexual activity. Of the women surveyed, 39 percent were virgins. I also got hold of two similar surveys, one a singles survey from Peachtree Presbyterian Church in Atlanta and the other a survey of single Southern Baptists. Both revealed only a third of the respondents had abstained from sex.[55]

Julia concludes that many single Christians, herself included, "see a celibate life as drab and full of suffering, like living somewhere between the Virgin Mary and Mother Theresa."[56] One reader who worked with college students wrote to tell me that some of them left their faith because of this issue, because they "saw singleness [and chastity] as a death sentence."

In this environment, a call to chastity may get the official Church nod, but it will likely be seen as the extreme, impractical, unattainable ideal by many Christians.

No Premarital Sex:
The Commandment-in-absentia

Upon cursory reading, the New Testament may appear to support this more lenient view. Believe it or not, the Bible never comes out and says directly, "Thou shalt not have sex before marriage." Premarital sex appears to be included in Paul's injunctions to avoid sexual immorality, in which he uses the Greek word *porneia*, from which we get *fornication*, but there's never any specific "don't do it before the wedding—or else!" command.

In First Corinthians 7, Paul's lengthy chapter on marriage, it's assumed that both the man and woman are physically pure when they marry. In Old Testament law, a woman who was not a virgin on her wedding night could be stoned to death. Other than that, it's not mentioned much in the Bible, though it is an assumed unspoken rule of life in many Bible stories.

It's fascinating that the main lesson modern evangelicals have taken from the Bible concerning purity is that we shouldn't have sex before marriage, considering the lack of emphasis the Bible actually places on this command.

A CALL TO PURITY:
THE HARDER BIBLICAL REALITY

Ah, yes—but wait. In the past, we've formed our conclusions about this area of life from what we *believe* the Bible says rather than what it *actually* says. We need to understand what it's actually saying.

The Bible's teaching on this subject mirrors Christ's words to His disciples: "You have heard that it was said to the people in the old days, 'Thou shalt not commit adultery.' But I say to you that every man who looks at a woman lustfully has already committed adultery with her—in his heart" (Mt. 5:27-28). We've been focused on trying not to cross that official sex-before-marriage line, when it seems that our actions become sinful. But the Bible's emphasis is not on premarital sex, but on something higher and harder to attain: purity.

Purity isn't a side issue. It's not something that we can compartmentalize away from the rest of our spiritual life. It affects who we are at our core, in ways that perhaps we don't fully understand.

THE BODY'S NEEDS

In First Corinthians, Paul challenges our assumptions about our bodies' needs and how they should be met:

> *But you cannot say that our physical body was made for sexual promiscuity; it was made for the Lord, and in the Lord is the answer to its needs. The God who raised the Lord from the dead will also raise us mortal men by His power. Have you not realised that your bodies are integral parts of Christ Himself? Am I then to take parts of Christ and join them to a prostitute? Never! Don't you realise that when a man joins himself to a prostitute he makes with her a physical unity? For, God says, "the two shall be one flesh." On the other hand the man who joins himself to the Lord is one with Him in spirit. Avoid sexual looseness like the plague! Every other sin that a man commits is done outside his own body, but this is an offence against his own body. Have you forgotten that your body is the temple of the Holy Spirit, who lives in you and is God's gift to you, and that you are not the owner of your own body? You have been bought, and at a price! Therefore bring glory to God in your body* (1 Corinthians 6:13-20).

Corinth was the Big Easy of its day, known for its temple to Aphrodite, where whoring substituted for worship. Imagine Paul writing this letter to the first-century Hugh Hefner, and you get the picture. To the Corinthians, sex was just another bodily appetite, like food—something the body needed, something that could be satiated without affecting one's spiritual state. Paul says not so.

Our bodies weren't made for sex, but for the Lord. "Sexual looseness," rather than filling our bodies' needs, mars our bodies and hinders them from achieving their true purpose.

There are two ways to read this passage. You could interpret it to mean that our bodies will find their ultimate fulfillment when God raises them from the dead, through the work of Christ. Or it could be saying that, in some way, the spiritual union with the Lord is the answer to our bodies' physical needs. One friend of mine has taken that leap of faith: "I don't know how, and this probably sounds crazy, but I know that God meets my needs, and I trust that He's capable—in some way unknown to me—of meeting these physical needs as well." Perhaps when we choose to follow the Lord in this regard, the spiritual reward in some way fulfills the physical needs.

Paul continues: Our bodies are no longer our own, really, having been paid for by Jesus' life. Now they are the dwelling place of the Holy Spirit, and, as such, worthy of honor and of more respect than lying around with prostitutes or any other kind of sexual indulgence. But something else he says catches my attention: our bodies are "integral parts of Christ Himself." We represent and are in fact the Body of Christ on earth. The Church—collectively, all of us humans who have found forgiveness and life in Christ—now in some way determine Christ's actions on earth. When we lust, when we give in, we cannot do so without bringing our little piece of the Body of Christ with us. We're no longer alone. And the sin that Paul claims to be an offense against a man's own body is also a stain upon the larger Body of which we're all a part.

Head to Foot

In Romans, Paul challenges us to be completely Christ's:

The night is nearly over, the day has almost dawned. Let us therefore fling away the things that men do in the dark, let us arm ourselves for the fight of the day! Let us live cleanly, as in the daylight, not in the delights of getting drunk or playing with sex, nor yet in quarrelling or jealousies. Let us be Christ's men from head to foot, and give no chances to the flesh to have its fling (Romans 13:12-14).

The New International Version translates verse 14 this way: "Rather, clothe yourselves with the Lord Jesus Christ, and do not think about how to gratify the desires of the sinful nature."

Paul invokes the imagery of war and the strong contrast of light and dark. There is no middle ground, Paul implies. We are either light or dark—playing with sex or living purely, giving in or arming ourselves for the fight. There is no question about where we ought to be and where all of our emotional energy should be directed: to the light. In that situation, we aren't thinking about our own needs or how we might be able to meet them somehow along the way. To be clothed with Christ, to be His completely, is to forget about ourselves in the light of the greater battle at hand.

After my relationship with Brian, this verse convicted me more than any other. What stood out to me was the fact that I was not thinking about serving Christ, about how to please Him. I thought only about myself—what I wanted and how much of it I could get. I wasn't clothed with Christ, nor was I His "from head to foot." I was a horrible mixture—serving my own passions, while trying to maintain some kind of service to God.

Becoming Like God

Christianity came out of Judaism and was largely a Jewish faith until Paul's missionary journeys expanded the faith among a wider audience. The church of Ephesus was one of the churches Paul planted—the believers there were Gentiles, not Jews, who didn't have the background of the Old Testament Law's moral code. Their personal histories were not necessarily religious or moral. Paul writes to them, encouraging them to live the new lives they've been given, to "become like God" rather than continuing to live in "lust's illusions":

> *This is my instruction, then, which I give you in the Lord's name. Do not live any longer the futile lives of gentiles. For they live in a world of shadows, and are cut off from the life of God....They have lost all decent feelings and abandoned themselves to sensuality, practising any form of impurity which lust can suggest. But you have learned nothing like that from Christ, if you have really heard His voice and understood the truth that Jesus has taught you. No, what you learned was to fling off the dirty clothes of the old way of living, which were rotted through and through with lust's illusions, and,*

with yourselves mentally and spiritually re-made, to put on the clean fresh clothes of the new life which was made by God's design for righteousness...So then you should try to become like God, for you are His children and He loves you. Live your lives in love—the same sort of love which Christ gave us and which He perfectly expressed when He gave Himself up for us as an offering and a sacrifice well-pleasing to God. But as for sexual immorality in all its forms, and the itch to get your hands on what belongs to other people—don't even talk about such things; they are no fit subjects for Christians to talk about (Ephesians 4:17-24; 5:1-3).

These believers had been "mentally and spiritually re-made"—they had new lives. Again, Paul draws clear distinctions. The old life is "dirty," "rotted through and through with lust's illusions," something to be flung away. The new life is "clean," "fresh," full of the love of God who considered them to be His children. Paul charges them to "try to become like God," a lofty goal made more reasonable by the greatness of His love for them. Part of becoming like God included abstaining from sexual immorality, but more than that, Paul instructed the believers in Ephesus not to even talk about it.

God's Command

If there were any doubt left about God's will in this area of our lives, any suspicion that these edicts come not from a loving God but from a church leadership anxious to burden people with guilt and shame, Paul clears it up in his first letter to the Thessalonians:

*God's plan is to make you holy, and that means a clean cut with sexual immorality. Every one of you should learn to control his body, keeping it pure and treating it with respect, and never allowing it to fall victim to lust, as do pagans with no knowledge of God. You cannot break this rule without cheating and exploiting your fellow-men....The calling of God is not to impurity but to the most thorough purity, and anyone who makes light of the matter is not making light of a man's ruling but of God's command. It is not for nothing that the Spirit God gives us is called the **Holy** Spirit (1 Thessalonians 4:3-8).*

Again, Paul draws clear distinctions between old and new, stressing that God calls us to "the most thorough purity," advising "a clean cut with sexual immorality." As if anticipating our doubt about the importance of this teaching, Paul equates rejecting this teaching with rejecting the God who gave it, saying that "anyone who makes light of the matter is not making light of a man's ruling but of God's command."

WHAT PURITY MEANS

So we know that God desires of us "the most thorough purity." What does that mean? It's obvious that sex before marriage is out, along with any substitutionary "entertain[ing] through other orifices." What about everything else? The Bible merely instructs us to be pure. We have to determine the specifics on our own. For me, it means allowing that side of my nature to be dormant for the time being, not that the desires aren't there, but as much as possible to let them sleep. It means living counterculturally, not only not crossing that "sex-before-marriage" line, but also directing my mind and heart to purity, to the light.

Repression?

The first impression one gets of this pure, chaste life is that of repression. Our culture teaches us that it is unnatural and unhealthy to leave these strong desires unfulfilled. Kathleen Norris, in *The Cloister Walk*, describes "the sexual idolatry of our culture": "The jiggle of tits and ass, penis and pectorals, assault us everywhere—billboards, magazines, television, movies. Orgasm becomes just another goal; we undress for success."[57] She describes the difficulty young celibates face amidst a culture that doesn't understand their desire to remain pure: "Often they find their loneliness intensified by the incomprehension of others. In a culture that denies the value of their striving, they are made to feel like fools, or worse."[58]

Such is our destiny, if we decide to pursue purity: to be made to feel foolish. And yet, we have to look at the source of this accusation: our own oversexed culture. In the book *A Return to Modesty*, which argues for chastity on practical, not religious grounds, author Wendy Shalit describes a culture in which fourth graders are taught about masturbation, sixth graders are surprised by a school's physical exams for genital herpes, and the only thing that shames a high schooler is not what she *has* done, but what she *hasn't*. In today's world, a bad reputation is a good thing. Shalit quotes *Cosmo* to show how far we have sunk: "Let's face it....In this age of instant gratification, there's something a little perverse about people who refuse to meet their deepest needs."[59]

Our culture is off balance. C.S. Lewis described our sexual instinct as having "gone wrong" from its original intent: to produce children. People can gather for a striptease, Lewis said, but were they to show the same enthusiasm for the slow revelation of a bit of mutton chop or bacon, you would know there was something wrong with their appetite for food. Along the same lines, we can assume there is something wrong with our sexual instinct when the sexual drive is so dominant in our culture.[60] So while our culture may view us as being dangerously repressed, that culture loses credibility to label us because its own sexual instincts are warped.

Lewis argues that the whole notion of repression is completely misunderstood in this context, that those of us who resist sexual desires are really in no danger of repressing them:

> …people often misunderstand what psychology
> teaches about 'repressions'. It teaches us that
> 'repressed' sex is dangerous. But 'repressed' is here
> a technical term: it does not mean 'suppressed' in
> the sense of 'denied' or 'resisted'. A repressed
> desire or thought is one which has been thrust into
> the subconscious (usually at a very early age) and
> can now come before the mind only in a disguised
> and unrecognisable form.…When an adolescent or
> adult is engaged in resisting a conscious desire, he
> is not dealing with a repression nor is he in the
> least danger of creating a repression. On the con-
> trary, those who are seriously attempting chastity
> are more conscious, and soon know a great deal
> more about their own sexuality than anyone else.
> They come to know their desires as Wellington
> knew Napoleon…[61]

Norris would agree with Lewis, saying that the Benedictine celibates she knows are neither infantile nor repressed, that "their struggles with celibacy have given them a truly sophisticated outlook on the subject of human sexuality..."[62] She notes that this kind of sexual discipline is necessary even in marriage:

> Like many people who came into adulthood during the sexually permissive 1960s, I've tended to equate sublimation with repression. But my celibate friends have helped me see the light; accepting sublimation as a normal part of adulthood makes me more realistic about human sexual capacities and expression. It helps me to respect the bonds and boundaries of marriage.
>
> Any marriage has times of separation, ill-health, or just plain crankiness, in which sexual intercourse is ill-advised. And it is precisely the skills of celibate friendship—fostering intimacy through letters, conversation, performing mundane tasks together (thus rendering them pleasurable), savoring the holy simplicity of a shared meal, or a walk together at dusk—that can help a marriage survive the rough spots. When you can't make love physically, you figure out other ways to do it.[63]

Writers often use the term *sublimation* instead of *repression* when referring to this commitment to chastity. We are not holding back, denying ourselves in a way that will cause lasting damage. Rather, we are taking a natural desire and refining it, giving it dignity, honor, and respect while keeping it in its proper place.

Pure Logistics

Although the Bible doesn't give us a set of detailed rules, it can be comforting to have your own guidebook when you're tackling something so big and seemingly unattainable as purity. Wendy Shalit describes the rules she set for herself in college:

> Suddenly, I decided, I would always leave the bedroom door open, I wouldn't see R-rated movies, I would always call men "Mister," and so on. People would ask me why I was making these rules for myself, and, frankly, I hadn't a clue. I think I sensed there was something I needed to protect—namely, my virginity—even though in public I knew it was something to be ashamed of, so privately I experienced more freedom in living within some limits, even if they had to be self-imposed.[64]

There are countless people in the Christian community who will give you a set of standards, but you have to decide what your own should be. You're the only one who knows what God requires of you in this area, the only one responsible for setting your own limits.

Josh Harris, in *I Kissed Dating Goodbye*, suggests that you completely avoid dating situations that would allow improper behavior, like being alone at one of your apartments to watch a movie or taking a backpacking trip together, alone. Josh suggests that you meet in public places—restaurants or parks—and that you try to spend time with friends and family.

Josh explains his reasoning:

We can only attain righteousness by doing two things—destroying sin in its embryonic stage and fleeing temptation....

...What does that look like? For me and many other people I know, it has meant rejecting typical dating. I go out with groups of friends; I avoid one-on-one dating because it encourages physical intimacy and places me in an isolated setting with a girl. Can't I handle it? Don't I have any self con- trol? Yeah, maybe I could handle it, but that's not the point. God says, "Flee the evil desires of youth, and pursue righteousness, faith, love and peace, along with those who call on the Lord out of a pure heart" (II Tim. 2:22). God is not impressed with my ability to stand up to sin. He's more impressed by the obedience I show when I run from it.[65]

Elisabeth Elliot's advice is succinct: "Keep your hands off and your clothes on."[66] In her words,

Why put yourself in any situation where the lines become smudged and obscure? Why take the risks? Why accept the pressure of tremendous temptation when you can easily avoid it by refus- ing to be anywhere where compromise is possible?[67]

For my own part, I've fallen back to a set of standards that not long ago seemed juvenile. I don't have dates over if we'll be in the house alone. I would prefer to wait until I'm engaged for that first kiss. (It's extreme, perhaps, but also hopelessly romantic. I can't help but picture Elizabeth and

Mr. Darcy in the final scene of *Pride and Prejudice*, when he leans over to kiss her as they ride off after their wedding. Every woman sighs at that spot in the movie. Our emotions betray us—deep down, we long for that kind of security in romantic expression.) I know myself. And perhaps that is the key to success here, and why this area is so personal and so different for each of us—we must each understand what purity requires of us. For me, I know, the simple innocent exchanges delved deeper into my heart and longings than I realized. These desires are easily awoken, and I would rather that they sleep for now.

This is the only way I know that I can be light instead of dark, be fully Christ's, be clean, avoid "lust's illusions," give my body to the Lord, and do my part with the small piece of the Body of Christ that is mine. Your answers may be different than mine—and that's fine. But know what your answers are.

If we are going to be successful, there are some mental and spiritual preparations as well, which Kathleen Norris hints at in her descriptions of Benedictine life. She tells of one Benedictine woman's insights on celibacy, given in a conference to her community:

> She depicted the celibate as extremely vulnerable in American culture, which promotes addictive behaviors. "Celibacy, like so much in the monastic life," she said, "is mostly a matter of paying attention. We have to be wary of anything that dulls conscious awareness, such as alcohol, or even television commercials."[68]

Another sister stressed the importance of prayer:

> One needs a deep prayer life to maintain a celibate
> life. It is only through prayer that the hard choices
> get made, over time, only prayer that can give me
> the self-transcendence that celibacy requires.[69]

Prayer, self-transcendence, paying attention to the world
around us, a guidebook of our own, a willingness to play the
fool from our culture's point of view—these are the keys to
our success.

A Good Reason

In her BreakPoint opinion piece, Julia Duin charged the
Church to come up with fresh reasons for chastity: "For post-
35 never-married and divorced people, it's not enough to tell
people to hang in there. When positive, fresh reasons are not
forthcoming, single evangelicals will be having sex."[70]

I don't know exactly how to answer that charge. Teen
chastity groups talk about the risks of STDs and pregnancy,
and while those are serious, you can minimize the risks if
you're careful and limit your number of partners. Girls are
warned that sex leads to emotional intimacy that will become
a gaping hole when the relationship ends. Although that risk
doesn't diminish with age, it may not seem so risky when the
alternative is to go back home to the house that's been empty
for 20-plus years and crawl into bed again alone. People who
teach chastity will tell you that the prospect of a fulfilling
marriage is one of the best motivations. When you're accept-
ing the reality that you may not get married or remarried,
what's your motivation then?

There's only one reason that can inspire you to purity in that situation: Jesus. He's not glamorous. He doesn't pound on the door and demand your attention. He sits quietly, knowing that you know He is there, waiting to see what your decision will be. He pleads with your heart.

I can't help but think that perhaps the reason Jesus' demands of us in this area seem so foreign to our everyday lives is that Jesus Himself is not really who we want Him to be. The Jews wanted a conquering hero to redeem them from Rome, not a peacenik carpenter who spoke in riddles about the value of the Kingdom of God. Today, we want Him to be sexy, charismatic, understanding of our weaknesses, cool enough to let things slide a little bit—a good Letterman guest, perhaps. He's none of those things.

And yet He is everything: Bread of Heaven, Redeemer, Morning Star, Creator, God-become-flesh. He is the One who bore our sins in His body, the One who died so that we would never know death's power, the One who purchased us from the grave. It is a well-worn analogy, but powerful nonetheless. We are His. He asks us to follow, and that is the only motivation that makes sense.

LIVING WITH FAILURE

If God's standards are high, we can be consoled by the fact that we need not fear failure. At least, when we fail, we have only to repent and return in order to be accepted, to start over again with no impunity. The depth of God's grace is enough to cover these sins, which have perhaps wrongly been made out by the Church to be worse than others.

And we can be sure that we are not alone in our struggles. Paul fought the control of sin (though not necessarily sexual sin) in his own life. In Romans 6, Paul talks about being "dead to sin" (verse 11, "...look upon yourselves as dead to the appeal and power of sin but alive to God through Christ Jesus our Lord"), but one chapter later he feels caught in its grasp:

> ...I am in hearty agreement with God's Law so far as my inner self is concerned. But then I find another law in my bodily members, which is in continual conflict with the Law which my mind approves, and makes me a prisoner to the law of sin which is inherent in my mortal body. For left to myself, I serve the Law of God with my mind, but in my unspiritual nature I serve the law of sin. It is an agonising situation, and who can set me free from the prison of this mortal body? I thank God there is a way out through Jesus Christ our Lord (Romans 7:21-25).

The Church has made such an issue out of virginity, and so adamantly portrays the effects of premarital sex (if you sleep with someone before you are married, you are more likely to divorce, less likely to have a good sex life, will be burdened with guilt—in general, your chances of a happy marriage are greatly diminished), that many who come to faith later in life feel like they failed before they began. They cannot undo what they've already done, and the Church makes them feel less Christian because they have a sexual past. The Bible never supports this. Many of the people Paul wrote to came to Christ out of a sordid past. It didn't matter. His response was always the same—"*And such were some of you!* But you have cleansed yourselves from all that, you have been made whole in spirit, you have been justified in the name of the Lord Jesus and in the Spirit of our God" (1 Cor. 6:11). What was darkness is now light; what was separate from God is now close to Him. The present is all that matters—the past is forgotten. We can be sure that God treats our own sordid histories the same way, and He no doubt can give us the grace to work through their effects on our lives.

THE DANGER OF GRACE

When so much grace is available, there is always the danger of its abuse—that we will look it in the face and proceed to do exactly what we want because we know it will be there for us when we're done. I know this always played into my decisions. I didn't want to displease God in this area, but I always knew that He would forgive me, so when I was faced with a difficult decision, I gave in, knowing that I could get rid of the guilt later. But my insides felt like they must be ugly to God. Paul addresses this idea in Romans 6: "Shall we sin to our heart's content and see how far we can exploit the grace of God? What a terrible thought! We, who have died to sin—how could we live in sin a moment longer?" (vv. 1-2).

Philip Yancey, in his book, *What's So Amazing About Grace*, says that the gamble we're taking in that kind of situation is not that God will forgive us, because we are always assured of that. We're gambling on ourselves—that we will want the forgiveness that is offered to us. Philip tells the story of being approached by a friend, Daniel, who decided to leave his wife and children after 15 years of marriage. He asked, "Do you think God can forgive something as awful as I am about to do?" Here is Philip's response:

Can God forgive you? Of course. You know the Bible. God uses murderers and adulterers. For goodness' sake, a couple of scoundrels named Peter and Paul led the New Testament church. Forgiveness is our problem, not God's. What we have to go through to commit sin distances us from God—we change in the very act of rebellion—and there is no guarantee we will ever come back. You ask me about forgiveness now, but will you even want it later, especially if it involves repentance?[71]

It turns out that Daniel didn't want the forgiveness God offered after he walked away from his marriage:

Several months after our conversation, Daniel made his choice and left his family. I have yet to see evidence of repentance. Now he tends to rationalize his decision as a way of escaping an unhappy marriage. He has branded most of his former friends "too narrow-minded and judgmental," and looks instead for people who celebrate his newfound liberation. To me, though, Daniel does not seem very liberated. The price of "freedom" has meant turning his back on those who cared about him most. He also tells me God is not part of his life right now. "Maybe later," he says.[72]

And that is the risk each of us take if we decide to sin and plan to come back to God when we're ready. We can't be assured that we will actually want God's grace when we need it.

LOVING THE LAW

I'm struck by how much I've come to dislike God's law in this area of life, to view it as a burden, an unnecessary constraint. I live in grace. I know that God forgives liberally and that He wants our hearts more than any perfunctory religious ceremony or bodily sign of devotion. And yet, He requires this bodily obedience, this sublimation of my desires, this backwardness, this humbling, with only the hope that the spiritual filling will in some way be an adequate replacement for the physical. Even having felt that spiritual fullness, I begrudge Him this standard.

I wonder if it is possible to love the purity God requires of us the way David loved God's law. He wrote in Psalm 19:

> *The law of the Lord is perfect, reviving the soul. The statutes of the Lord are trustworthy, making wise the simple. The precepts of the Lord are right, giving joy to the heart. The commands of the Lord are radiant, giving light to the eyes. The fear of the Lord is pure, enduring forever. The ordinances of the Lord are sure and altogether righteous. The are more precious than gold, than much pure gold; they are sweeter than honey, than honey from the comb. By them is your servant warned; in keeping them there is great reward* (Psalm 19:7-11).

In Psalm 119, he speaks of a soul "consumed with longing for Your laws at all times" (v. 20), of finding delight in God's law, of rising at midnight to praise Him for it, of knowing it to be of greater value than wealth. And, in verse 18, he prays a prayer that I echo:

> *Open my eyes that I may see wonderful things in Your law.*

Chapter Nine

YOU CAN CHANGE THE WAY
YOU FEEL ABOUT BEING SINGLE

࿋

Before Bridget Jones came along, I worried that I was crazy. Granted, a fictional character is not necessarily sound for purposes of comparison, but I felt better to think that perhaps I was not the only one who had temporary moments of insanity in which I imagined myself to be completely beyond anyone's ability to love—a horrible old spinster with no life, no friends, no love interests, and probably some glaring defect that those close to me are too kind to point out but that shouts my insufficiency to any man who comes within 30 feet. It comforted me to think I'm not quite as bad off as Bridget because I never imagined the part about dying alone, eaten by a pack of wild dogs.

Temporary moments of insanity aside, singleness traps some in a tomb of depression from which it seems impossible to escape. One early-30's single thought God was not only denying her fulfillment, but flaunting the fact that He was giving others what she wanted. She concluded that her best bet was for a quick end to it all. She wrote this to me:

> I believed God had a plan for me like everyone else. Mine looked something like this—working in ministry with teens with my spouse, having children, etc. Well I have worked with teens in ministry but no longer am....

> ...what happened is that I got so frustrated, I let it all go. I did become bitter with God primarily because I saw everyone else's dream being fulfilled but mine. I even believed that God was bringing people into my life to show me the reality of my dream coming to pass. For example, I met a young couple who work together in ministry. I have really withdrawn and left my home church....

> I have one question for you. Did you ever in your life find yourself hoping that God would take you home soon?...

> I guess what I am trying to say is that the hope I try to hold onto everyday is that this pain is for a short time. One day Jesus will come. I am just trying to find purpose somewhere.

A divorcée wrote to me about the cumulative pain of years of self-sufficiency, of dealing with friends who had no idea how to help her or what to say, of hearing the Church condemn divorce over and over when her manic depressive, bisexual husband had left her no choice:

...going to church leaves me crying and sad, all those happy couples and happy families....I am just tired, lonely, sad that I have no one to share my children and my joys and sadness with....The biggest thing is that I feel I am not worthy of having someone love me for who I am...there must be something I am learning here...that we should put on a happy face...should just get over it.

Is it possible to feel differently? One self-described "frustrated and angry single woman" wrote to tell me that she was at the end of her rope. She didn't want to be angry and bitter, but she was. She agreed that trials bring us closer to God, but, she said, "I can't stop the way I feel." Perhaps that's what we all believe about our feelings. Things happen to us, good things and bad, and the natural response is to feel happy or sad, secure or lonely. Continual reminders of a broken heart and unfulfilled expectations can make you terrifyingly depressed. These feelings are natural, and there's nothing that can be done about them. Or is there?

LIFE IN YOUR HEAD

"Your feelings don't run your life. Your mind should be in charge. Most people don't understand that. They don't believe they can control what they're feeling. In fact, what you believe determines what you think, what you feel, and how you act. If you change your beliefs, your life will change. Most of your life happens in your head."

Lee Darcy, a friend and Christian counselor, uses cognitive therapy to help people change their lives. She sat across from me at La Madeleine, drinking coffee and explaining to me the way our thoughts and feelings are connected.

All of us have been gathering truths about the world since we were small. We try to categorize things, and figure out the rules of the game, to make our lives more comprehensible. Our assumptions become internalized. Our thinking patterns become habitual, until we have fairly consistent ways of thinking about a given topic. When we encounter a given situation, our automatic thought process kicks in. You probably don't even realize that you do this, but you do. It's called self-talk.

None of this is wrong; it's the way God made us. The problem is that often these thinking patterns contain lies about ourselves and the world around us. The lies in our self-talk lead to anxiety and depression.

Psychologist and author Dr. Chris Thurman, in his book *The Lies We Believe*, compares self-talk to "tapes that hold all the beliefs, attitudes, and expectations that you have 'recorded' during your life."[73] These tapes play over and over in our minds, though we're often unconscious of it—life presses the play button for us. He also compares these automatic thoughts to a computer program that's launched when we encounter certain situations. The lies we believe are like bugs in the program; the error they produce is our depression and angst.

For example, if you've grown up believing the American philosophy that money is success, you'll be distraught at the possibility of having to take a lower-paying job in the midst of a difficult economy. You may think you're a failure for having to take a pay cut—you may not feel better until your prospects improve. Or if your generous frame doesn't fit the "beauty is thin" mantra you've been fed all your life, you may feel less deserving of friendship, romance, and attention. Deep inside, your thoughts are askew. You believe that beautiful people deserve good things—the beautiful people who are thin and tanned and have a perfect Roman nose. You are none of these things, so you tell yourself that you are less of a person, less valuable, not as promising as a Ralph Lauren model or a size 6 would be.

Or, if you believe you should have married long ago, the fifth wedding invitation in a month may send you into despair. Dr. William Backus, in his book *Telling Yourself the Truth*, offers this example:

> The depressed person believes he or she can never be happy without the thing they now do not possess. Jennifer tells herself that she will never know true happiness if she doesn't get married. Many single people suffer with this misbelief. "Only through marriage can I experience life fully." If that sentence follows with, "I'll never get married. Nobody will ever love me," there's trouble. "All I can expect from life is frustration and unfulfillment" will be the words in the person's self-talk."[74]
> We may not be quick to connect the problem to our thoughts instead of to our circumstances. It seems logical to think that a bevy of marital bliss among your close acquaintances would send you into a tailspin. (And, certainly, that would make anyone

struggle.) But there are probably lies at the root of that depression. You may believe this is proof that God has abandoned you and does not meet your needs the way He promised. You may wonder what you have done wrong to be passed over. You may think that to be the one person among your acquaintances who has not been chosen is a slap in the face, something to be ashamed of. These ideas seep from lies that have planted themselves in your mind and become entrenched there over time.

Our self-talk sounds true to us. We don't deliberately lie to ourselves; we've believed these things for so long we don't recognize that they aren't true. Dr. Backus blames this deceit on satan: "...the misbeliefs we tell ourselves are directly from the pit of hell. They are hand engraved and delivered by the devil himself. He is very clever in dishing out misbeliefs. He doesn't want to risk being discovered so he always appears as if the lie he is telling us is true."[75]

Jesus confirmed this character quality of satan's in John 8:44: " 'Your father is the devil, and what you are wanting to do is what your father longs to do. He always was a murderer, and has never dealt with the truth, since the truth will have nothing to do with him. Whenever he tells a lie, he speaks in character, for he is a liar and the father of lies.' "

THE BATTLE IN YOUR MIND

The way we think—what we believe at our core being—about our singleness determines how we feel about being single. I'm convinced that the key to life is not what happens to you or how you respond to it, as the old adage goes, but the way you think about it. Our thoughts are truth or error, life or death. We imagine sometimes that we are trapped in these feelings of worthlessness, of depression—we cannot see our way out. But there is a way.

My friend Lee continued her explanation to me:

Your heart is a garden. You've been planting seeds your whole life; some of them you've planted, some of them others have planted for you. In order to change, you have to figure out which ones are weeds and then substitute the truth for the lies.

Because this process is habitual, it's possible to change. But it's difficult. It takes time. You have to expect it to take time.

First, you have to take every thought captive. Recognize what you are telling yourself. Examine your thoughts and feelings. What fundamental belief of yours is responsible for what you are feeling? Is it true?

Second, tear down strongholds. When you identify a lie, break it down. Tell yourself it's not true, and why.

Third, replace the lie with the truth. This step is absolutely crucial. Unless you put the truth in, you leave a void in your heart that satan can fill with more untruths.

To help me track my progress, she sketched out a chart originally developed by psychologist Albert Ellis. It has five columns. In the first column, I write the situation that triggers feelings of anxiety or emotional distress (i.e., friend's wedding). In the second I put the self-talk, or lie, that is the root cause for those feelings (God has forgotten me). In the third column I say what I'm feeling, along with a degree of emotional intensity, from 1 to 100 (depression, anger, shame, 75). Then in the fourth column I write the truth that will replace the lie (God guides me. He watches over me carefully. He has not forgotten me). In the fifth column I outline emotions again, along with the new level of intensity (depression, anger, shame, 50). Lee cautions, "The feelings will still be there, but they should be less intense. Your emotions won't change automatically. You may think you're doing something wrong because your bad feelings are still there. But those feelings should gradually lessen with time." I wonder how long this chart would be if I were to root out all the lies in my head.

Lee continues:

This process is volitional. You have to choose to change. You have to choose to recognize these automatic thoughts and believe that they're not true. You may think you can change your belief patterns overnight simply by exposing yourself to the truth. But you have to really believe the new truth. You can know something is true intellectually, but not believe that it's true at the core of your being. That's where you need to be—believing it at the core.

You have to argue with yourself. This is a battle in your mind.

Dr. Thurman reminds us that in order to arrive at actual truth, we have to use God as our starting point. If we rely solely on advice from family, friends, even ministry leaders, we'll be subject to falling for lies again because our friends and family are just as susceptible to believing a lie as we are.[76] He also cautions that the process takes a long time, and that, in the beginning, trying to replace lies with truth can be more painful than just living with the lies you're used to. In time, though, the rewards are great.[77]

One thing all of these advisers make clear: our emotional health depends on our thoughts being full of truth. To the extent that we believe lies, we'll suffer accordingly.

KEEPING YOUR MIND

The Bible talks a lot about the power of what we put in our hearts and minds, and it urges us to seek wisdom and truth. The teacher in Proverbs exhorts the young men in his charge to keep his instruction in their hearts, and—whatever else they do in life—to acquire wisdom:

When I was a boy in my father's house, still tender, and an only child of my mother, he taught me and said, "Lay hold of my words with all your heart; keep my commands and you will live. Get wisdom, get understanding; do not forget my words or swerve from them. Do not forsake wisdom, and she will protect you; love her, and she will watch over you. Wisdom is supreme; therefore get wisdom. Though it cost all you have, get understanding. Esteem her, and she will exalt you; embrace her, and she will honor you. She will set a garland of grace on your head and present you with a crown of splendor" (Proverbs 4:3-9).

Paul provides a prescription for a healthy thought life in Philippians 4:

> *Delight yourselves in the Lord, yes, find your joy in Him at all times....Don't worry over anything whatever; whenever you pray tell God every detail of your needs in thankful prayer, and the peace of God, which surpasses human understanding, will keep constant guard over your hearts and minds as they rest in Christ Jesus. My brothers, I need only add this. If you believe in goodness and if you value the approval of God, **fix your minds on whatever is true and honourable and just and pure and lovely and admirable** (Philippians 4:4-8).*

Paul describes our task in Second Corinthians (although, in context, he may have been referring more to the battles of apologetics than to those necessary to discipline our own minds):

> *Our battle is to break down every deceptive argument and every imposing defence that men erect against the true knowledge of God. We fight to capture every thought until it acknowledges the authority of Christ* (2 Corinthians 10:4-5).

When Paul describes the armor of God that will help defeat "the unseen power that controls this dark world, and spiritual agents from the very headquarters of evil" in Ephesians 6, the first piece he lists is the belt of truth. He tells us that our battles are spiritual, not physical, and that our weapons are different than any his first-century readers may have been accustomed to using. He says the armor is necessary to resist "the devil's craftiness" (v. 11), a characteristic

C.S. Lewis captured in Screwtape's devotion to "undermining faith and preventing the formation of virtues."[78]

Our hearts and minds are under assault. Our defense is to constantly seek to fill them with truth.

LIES & TRUTH

When I began this book, I was not content and wondered why God had given me the life He had. But I sensed, somehow, in spite of my confusion, that the life I'd been given was good. I desperately wanted to believe that God had a plan, that I was not a freak or a failure.

A lifetime of soaking up evangelical thought had not prepared me for this. It had introduced me to a God who met our needs—as we define them (material possessions, family, good things) rather than as He defines them (a character like Christ, a knowledge of Him)—who blessed us when we were good, who was always looking out for His own. It had not prepared me for serving God and finding great disappointment. Perhaps that's because I wasn't listening or thought that these things only happened to other people, or was too immature to hear that lesson.

But in my late 20s, this great disappointment met me one evening when I was curled up on the couch with my soon-to-be-ex-boyfriend and not-to-be-fiancé. It followed me around, tagging along at work, at church, at holiday parties, and at family dinners. I tried to avoid it, hoping it would go away, but there was no health in that. So I determined to stare it down, to swallow it whole, to dig into it and find what was valuable at the core. I wanted to rebuild my mind—and my image—with truth.

The book has been a struggle to search out the truth: You may not get married. You're right where God wants you to be. You have no reason to be ashamed. Marriage isn't heaven. You are loved. You can be content.

Here are the truth and lies we've examined, in summary:

Lies	Truth
God has someone out there for me.	*God may or may not have someone for me to marry. Either way, He is sovereign, and it is His decision. He knows what is best for me and for His eternal plan.*
It's wrong for me to still be single. I must have done something wrong.	*My singleness isn't my failure. It's a good part of part of God's plan for me and nothing to be ashamed of or feel guilty about.*
I've missed God's plan for my life.	*God's will doesn't work that way. Nowhere in the Bible does it say that if I take one wrong step God's plan for my life will be ruined forever. In the end, He's more concerned about the state of my heart than the specific life choices—where to work, where to live—I make.*
God must have something more to teach me.	*Singleness isn't the school for the biblically inept. Marriage is not a reward for spiritual maturity.*
Married life is inherently better than single life.	*Married life isn't necessarily better or worse (though it can be both). It's just different, with different blessings and different challenges.*

Lies	Truth
I am not loved.	*God loves me fiercely. I couldn't escape His love if I tried. His love, however, has greater designs on my life than my own happiness. As God's creation, His work, He wants to build in me a certain character. He gives me what He knows I need in order to become the person I need to be.*
I cannot be content.	*Contentment is a spiritual discipline that takes time, but it's possible. It's a decision, not a feeling, and it's not dependent on what I have.*
It's not fair for God to ask me to abstain from sex.	*Purity is essential to my spiritual health. It's not up to me to decide what's fair—Christ has called me to pursue purity, and so I follow. He welcomes me with open arms when I fail and come back to Him.*

I've been at this for a while, and my thinking is changing, but there are still lies skirting about the corners and occasionally taking center stage. I pray that our lives will be transformed by truth—that we will stop feeling less valuable, stop focusing on our singleness, and live in light of the blessings God's given us and the role He allows us to play in His Kingdom.

Be kind to yourself. Recognize that this is going to take time. Celebrate every small step in the right direction.

Chapter Ten

IT'S NOT ALL ABOUT THIS LIFE: IT'S ABOUT THE ETERNAL

❧

Christianity is otherworldly, meaning it is essentially about another world. God is from that other world. He created ours. When we were lost and sinful and stupid, He came into our world to save us from ourselves, from satan, from the effects of our sin. We don't understand His world. We can't see it, though it may surround us, and perhaps at times we sense some kind of otherworldly presence—angels, light, peace. It is our final destination, this other world—something we call "eternal life," although since it is outside of time and space, the concept of an eternity does not really exist there, since there is no time, and if no time, then really no forever (at least, the way we imagine forever).

We get glimpses into this other world—pictures of angels ascending and descending a ladder; Jesus on a throne, in glory, shining down to give peace to a dying martyr. We understand that there are battles there between good and evil. And our actions somehow affect these otherworldly battles.

Stakes may be waged, as with Job, on what our reactions will be, on whether or not we continue to believe, continue to praise.

Everything that Jesus taught makes sense only in light of this other world: Give up your life, wealth doesn't matter, power doesn't matter. Put on a towel and wash someone's feet. Follow Me. If you have to, in order to follow Me, give up everything that is important to you.

Varied imagery has arisen through the years to capture our plight as people who do not belong to the world they are in and cannot imagine the one to which they are headed. We are pilgrims, strangers, aliens, not of this world.

Yet, we live every day here. We buy blue jeans and run to the grocery store to pick up a roast chicken for dinner because we don't have time to cook. We have dreams—to travel, to buy a new couch for the family room, to report to the CEO, to be the CEO.

And those of us who are single dream about being loved and being married.

The extent to which we're content being single will be determined by how much we really believe about this other world that Christianity presents.

Two years ago, on Labor Day, I sat in the September sun with Harry Potter and a fever, nursing a sore throat. I ended up in the emergency room at 3 a.m., unable to swallow, my throat was so sore. Weeks later, still lethargic, the doctors could only diagnose my problem as "a mono-like virus." I missed several weeks of work before I could go back part-time, and I wasn't full-time again until January. I was on a hiatus from life. I was starved and exhausted and running a fever. I could do nothing normal—work, laundry, getting the lasagna unstuck from the dinner dishes before putting them in the sink—so I read. On my yellow corduroy couch, in bed, or sitting on my green plastic adirondack chair in the afternoon sun. I finished the Harry Potter series, re-read all the Narnia books, and ate up *The Lord of the Rings*.

My real world was a haze, so I lost myself in Hogwarts, Narnia, and Middle-Earth. The idea of another world became very real to me. Not that I expected to start receiving letters by owl post or walk through a wardrobe to meet Tumnus, but I became more open to things not really being as they seem, to an underlying reality that may be incomprehensible and often unnoticed.

Jesus, before He was crucified, told the disciples that they would go through an incredibly difficult time—similar to that of a woman going into labor. Eventually, though, they would see Jesus again and would forget their pain:

> I tell you truly that you are going to be both sad and sorry while the world is glad. Yes, you will be deeply distressed, but your grief will turn into joy. When a woman gives birth to a child, she knows grievous pain when her time comes. Yet as soon as she has given birth to the child, she no longer remembers her agony for joy that a man has been born into the world. Now you are going through pain, but I shall see you again and your hearts will thrill with joy—the joy that no one can take away from you—and on that day you will not ask Me any questions (John 16:20-23a).

The Single Truth

We may not get what we want. Our lives may be difficult—though we are blessed in so many ways. But at some point we will see Jesus, and our life here will be a dim memory. We will be full of joy. The denials and sacrifices God asks of us here are of little consequence, in light of that.

ENDNOTES

1. Dr. Larry Crabb, Interview with author. "Dr. Larry Crabb on Shattered Dreams," August 7, 2001, Crosswalk.com: http://women.crosswalk.com/CC/CDA/CC_Content/CC_Archive_Display_Page/0,,PTID73970 | CHID200054 | GRPID6 231,00.html

2. Madeleine L'Engle, *Two-Part Invention: The Story of a Marriage* (San Francisco: HarperSanFrancisco, 1989), 123-125.

3. Thanks to John MacMurray for these thoughts on the story of Hananiah, Mishael, and Azariah, taken from his teaching at the Reston Bible Church Single Focus retreat in October of 1997.

4. Fyodor Dostoyevsky, *The Brothers Karamazov*, trans. David Magarshack (London: Penguin Books, 1982), 26.

5. Kathleen Norris, *The Cloister Walk* (New York: Riverhead Books, 1996), 35, 45.

6. Elisabeth Elliot, *God's Guidance: A Slow and Certain Light* (Grand Rapids, Michigan: Fleming H. Revell, 1997), 30.

7. Ibid, 63.

8. Ibid, 65.

9. Thomas Merton, *Dialogues with Silence*, ed. Jonathan Montaldo (San Francisco: HarperSanFrancisco, 2001), vii. Originally appeared in Thomas Merton, Thoughts in Solitude (New York: Farrar, Straus & Cudahy, 1958), 101.

10. Garry Friesen with J. Robin Maxson, *Decision Making and the Will of God: A Biblical Alternative to the Traditional View* (Portland, Oregon: Multnomah Press, 1980), 15.

11. Ibid, 32-33.

12. Ibid, 162.

13. M. Blaine Smith, *Knowing God's Will: Finding Guidance for Personal Decisions* (Downers Grove, Illinois: InterVarsity Press, 1991), 123.

14. Elisabeth Elliot, *Quest for Love: True Stories of Passion and Purity* (Grand Rapids, Michigan: Fleming H. Revell, 1996), 215.

15. Albert Hsu, *Singles at the Crossroads: A Fresh Perspective on Christian Singleness* (Downers Grove, Illinois: InterVarsity Press, 1997), 58.

16. "A *HIS* Interview with John R. W. Stott," *HIS* (October 1975), 19, as cited in Hsu, *Singles at the Crossroads*, 77.

17. Hsu, *Singles at the Crossroads*, 78.

18. Elliot, *God's Guidance*, 13.

19. Bebo Norman, "The Hand I've Been Dealt," ChristianityToday.com, February 20, 2002 <http://www.christianitytoday.com/singles/newsletter/mind20220.html>.

20. Albert Hsu, *Singles at the Crossroads: A Fresh Perspective on Christian Singleness* (Downers Grove, Illinois: InterVarsity Press, 1997), 24.

21. Helen Fielding, *Bridget Jones's Diary* (New York: Penguin Books, 1996), 35.

22. Ibid, 37.

23. Hsu, *Singles at the Crossroads*, 32-33. Quoting Rodney Clapp, *Families at the Crossroads* (Downers Grove, Illinois: InterVarsity Press, 1993), 95.

24. K.C. Hanson and Douglas E. Oakman, *Palestine at the Time of Jesus: Social Structures and Social Conflicts* (Minneapolis: Fortress Press, 1998), 31.

25. Hsu, *Singles at the Crossroads*, 35.

26. Ibid, 25-26.

27. Hanson and Oakman, *Palestine*, 43.

28. Hsu, *Singles at the Crossroads*, 38.

29. Ibid, 37.

30. Ibid, 36.

31. Eugene H. Peterson, *The Message: The New Testament Psalms and Proverbs in Contemporary Language* (Colorado Springs, CO: NavPress, 1993), 350.

32. Garry Friesen with J. Robin Maxson, *Decision Making and the Will of God: A Biblical Alternative to the Traditional View* (Portland, Oregon: Multnomah Press, 1980), 293-294.

33. Hsu, *Singles at the Crossroads*, 81.

34. C.S. Lewis, *A Grief Observed* (New York: Bantam Books, 1963), 20.

35. Ibid, 55-56.

36. *Good Will Hunting* (Miramax: 1997), directed by Gus Van Sant, written by Matt Damon and Ben Affleck.

37. David James Duncan, *The Brothers K* (New York: Bantam Books, 1992), 212.

38. *Enchanted April* (1992), directed by Mike Newell, based on the novel by Elizabeth von Arnim.

39. William Backus and Marie Chapian, *Telling Yourself the Truth* (Minneapolis: Bethany House, 1980), 31.

40. Dennis Rainey, general editor, et al., *Preparing for Marriage: The Complete Guide to Help You Discover God's Plan for a Lifetime of Love* (Ventura, California: Gospel Light, 1997), 8.

41. Jill Bartlett, "The Reasons We're Thankful: Christian authors and performers share what they're most thankful for this holiday season," November 2001, Crosswalk.com: http://family.crosswalk.com/partner/Article_Display_Page/0,,PTID74451%7CCHID233672%7CCIID1108678,00.html

42. Henri Nouwen, *Clowning in Rome* (New York: Doubleday, 1979), quoted in Robert Durback, ed., *Seeds of Hope: A Henri Nouwen Reader* (New York: Doubleday, 1997), 72.

43. "There's a Wideness in God's Mercy," words by Frederick Faber, music by John Austin, 2000, Austin Echo Music, on the CD *Hymns*.

44. Madeleine L'Engle, *A Live Coal in the Sea* (San Francisco: HarperSanFrancisco, 1996), 167.

45. Anne Lamott, *Traveling Mercies: Some Thoughts on Faith* (New York: Anchor Books, 1999), 49.

46. C.S. Lewis, *The Problem of Pain* (New York: Touchstone, 1962), 35-36.

47. Ibid, 38, 48.

48. Lamott, *Traveling Mercies*, 7-8.

49. Lewis, *Problem of Pain*, 107.

50. Ibid, 41-42.

51. This prayer first came to me through the e-mail discussion group of Kairos, the young adult group at Falls Church Episcopal in Falls Church, Virginia. It is available online at the website of the Spiritual Family of Charles de Foucauld <http://www.jc.gn.apc.org/ador-desert/abandon.shtm>.

52. Elisabeth Elliot, *Passion and Purity: Bring your love life under Jesus Christ's control* (Old Tappan, New Jersey: Fleming H. Revell Company, 1984), 12.

53. Lauren F. Winner, "Sex and the Single Evangelical: The church lady vs. the 'evangelical whore'," Beliefnet.com: <http://www.beliefnet.com/story/5/story_597_1.html>.

54. Barna Research Online, "Practical Outcomes Replace Biblical Principles as the Moral Standard," September 10, 2001 <http://www.barna.org/cgi-bin/PagePressRelease.asp?Press ReleaseID=97&Reference=B>.

55. Julia Duin, "No One Wants to Talk About It: Why are evangelical singles sleeping around?" BreakPoint.org <http: //www.breakpoint.org/Breakpoint/ChannelRoot/Features Group/OnlineFeatures/No+One+Wants+to+Talk+About+It. htm>.

56. Ibid.

57. Kathleen Norris, *The Cloister Walk* (New York: Riverhead Books, 1996), 117.

58. Ibid.

59. Wendy Shalit, *A Return to Modesty: Discovering the Lost Virtue* (New York: The Free Press, 1999), 187, as cited in Jenny Lombard, "Let's face it: How to stay single FOREVER," *Cosmopolitian*, June 1994.

60. C.S. Lewis, *Mere Christianity* (San Francisco: HarperSanFrancisco, 1952), 96-97.

61. Ibid, 102.

62. Norris, *Cloister Walk*, 259-260.

63. Ibid, 118.

64. Shalit, *A Return to Modesty: Discovering the Lost Virtue*, 190.

65. Joshua Harris, *I Kissed Dating Goodbye: A New Attitude Toward Romance and Relationships* (Sisters, Oregon: Multnomah Books, 1997), 95.

66. Elisabeth Elliot, *Quest for Love: True Stories of Passion and Purity* (Grand Rapids, Michigan: Fleming H. Revell, 1996), 269.

67. Elliot, *Passion and Purity*, 147.

68. Norris, *Cloister Walk*, 260.

69. Ibid, 261.

70. Duin, "No One Wants to Talk About It."

71. Philip Yancey, *What's So Amazing About Grace* (Grand Rapids, Michigan: Zondervan Publishing House, 1997), 180.

72. Ibid, 180.

73. Dr. Chris Thurman, *The Lies We Believe: The #1 Cause of Our Unhappiness* (Nashville: Thomas Nelson, 1989), 22-23, 187.

74. William Backus and Marie Chapian, *Telling Yourself the Truth* (Minneapolis: Bethany House, 1980), 44-45.

75. Ibid, 18.

76. Thurman, *The Lies We Believe: The #1 Cause of Our Unhappiness*, 166-167.

77. Ibid, 177-183.

78. C.S. Lewis, *The Screwtape Letters* (San Francisco: Harper San Francisco, 1942), 22.

For more information on Lori's writing and speaking ministry, including contact information, please visit her website at **www.thesingletruth.org**

Additional copies of this book and other
book titles from DESTINY IMAGE are
available at your local bookstore.

For a complete list of our titles,
visit us at www.destinyimage.com
Send a request for a catalog to:

Destiny Image₀ Publishers, Inc.

P.O. Box 310
Shippensburg, PA 17257-0310

*"Speaking to the Purposes of God for This
Generation and for the Generations to Come"*